Praise for the *Earth Spirit* series

There is no doubt that this world is in crisis. The ecological and sociological reality we're living in and must face up to is quite frankly terrifying. Yet there is hope. The authors of the *Earth Spirit* series from Moon Books show us that there are solutions to be found in ecological and eco-spiritual practices. I recommend this series to anyone who is concerned about our current situation and wants to find some hope in solutions they can practice for themselves.
Sarah Kerr, Pagan Federation President

This bold and rich *Earth Spirit* series provides vital information, perspectives, poetry and wisdom to guide and support through the complex environmental, climate and biodiversity challenges and crisis facing us all. Nothing is avoided within the wide range of author views, expertise and recommendations on eco-spirituality. I am deeply inspired by the common call, across the books, to radically change our relatio_____ he planet to a more respectful, mu'_____ way of living; both individually a_____ 'fers its own particular flavour a_____ ıs and ways forward in these un_____ .ıy the series provides an innovativ_____ and compelling compendium of how to live, hope and act from both ancient and modern wisdoms. Whatever your views, concerns and aspirations for your life, and for the planet, you will find something of value. My life and understanding is deeply enhanced through the privilege of reading this series.
Dr Lynne Sedgmore CBE, Founder of Goddess Luminary Leadership Wheel, Executive Coach, Priestess and ex Chief Executive

In a world that is faced with such immense environmental issues, we can often feel paralysed and impotent. The *Earth Spirit* series is a welcome and inspiring antidote to fear and apathy. These books gift us with positive and inspiring visions that serve to empower and strengthen our own resolve to contribute to the healing of our planet, our communities and ourselves.
Eimear Burke, Chosen Chief of The Order of Bards, Ovates and Druids

Thanks to Moon Books and an amazing group of authors for stepping up in support of our need to address, with grace and aliveness, the ecological crises facing humanity. We must take concerted, focused, positive action on every front NOW, and this is best and most powerfully done when we base our offerings in a deep sense of spirit. White Buffalo Woman came to us 20 generations ago, reminding us of the importance of a holy perception of the world - based in Oneness, unity, honor and respect. Even as that is profound, it is also practical, giving us a baseline of power from which to give our gifts of stewardship and make our Earth walk a sacred one - for us and for All Our Relations. Walk in Beauty with these authors!
Brooke Medicine Eagle, Earthkeeper and author of *Buffalo Woman Comes Singing* and *The Last Ghost Dance*

Earth Spirit is an exciting and timely series. It has never been more important to engage with ideas that promote a positive move forward for our world. Our planet needs books like these - they offer us heartening signposts through the most challenging of times.
Philip Carr-Gomm, author of *Druid Mysteries, Druidcraft* and *Lessons in Magic*

This is important work as we humans face one of the greatest challenges in our collective history.

Ellen Evert Hopman, Archdruid of Tribe of the Oak and author of *A Legacy of Druids, A Druid's Herbal of Sacred Tree Medicine, The Sacred Herbs of Spring,* and other volumes

Our relationship to the Mother Earth and remembering our roles as caretakers and guardians of this sacred planet is essential in weaving ourselves back into the tapestry of our own sacred nature. From the shamanic perspective, we are not separate from nature. The journey to finding solutions for the Earth will come through each person's reconnection to her heartbeat and life force.

Chandra Sun Eagle, author of *Looking Back on the Future*

What people are saying about

Confronting the Crisis

David Sparenberg's *Earth Spirit: Confronting the Crisis* is an invaluable wisdom book. Divided equally between its two parts, the 11 essays in part one explore this relevant and timely subject from different angles and in various forms. Inclined towards posing deep questions, David Sparenberg inspires and invites the reader to dialogue and find their own answers and solutions. It is with the 20 inspirational meditations of part two, however, that we are invited to experience the full eloquence, spiritual power and deep wisdom of the author.

David Sparenberg is a dreamer in the shamanic tradition of pathfinders and an eco-poet in heart and soul, which shows throughout the book as he envisions approaches to our collectively creating a culture where humans mature into avatars of relationships. While honestly addressing subjects of challenge and urgency, Sparenberg invites us to democratize alternative forms of education, culture and communities based on responsibility, appreciation and diversity delight. Frequently he asks the reader to listen more intently, feel more deeply, awaken their senses to think anew, and unite with others making choices working toward sustainable change.

David Sparenberg, who is a dogma-free seeker and latter-day eco-spirituality troubadour, believes that instead of facing species extinction, with dedication, imagination, and discipline we can enter a values renaissance for the combined future of Earth and Humanity.

Christa Mackinnon (MSc), Author of *Shamanism and Spirituality in Therapeutic Practice* and *Shamanism: Awaken and Develop the Shamanic Force Within*

David Sparenberg writes about the collective crisis the earth is facing which may lead to the end of our species and most other species on earth. He says that we human species are at war with nature. This is a recipe for collective doom. However, his writings are not all gloom and doom. He draws upon the collective spirituality of human civilization to find solutions to the quagmire we are in. He invites us to dialogue and prompts us to seek counter-solutions. These counter-solutions may be found in the wisdom of our ancestors which are now cherished by our indigenous brethren. Seeking, discussing and practicing indigenous spirituality will give us clue to a new path towards a new beginning, a beginning which will lead us towards a new horizon of peace, justice and harmony which will regenerate our civilization and solve most of our problems. David Sparenberg's writings are meditative and poetic. Reading his articles lift us to a new realm of hope. In a world where there is so much gloom and doom the hope that Sparenberg's articles impart is something to be cherished.

Binu Mathew, Editor, Countercurrents.org

During these difficult times of turbulence we need more than ever a voice of hope and guidance, a voice of awareness and spirituality. David Sparenberg is exactly that; a voice of healing, of consciousness, of hope, of ecosophy, of friendship.

Thanos Kalamidas, Editor in Chief, Ovi magazine & Ovi project

EARTH SPIRIT

Confronting the Crisis

Essays and Meditations on
Eco-Spirituality

Eᴀʀᴛʜ Sᴘɪʀɪᴛ

Confronting the Crisis

Essays and Meditations on
Eco-Spirituality

David Sparenberg

MOON
BOOKS
Winchester, UK
Washington, USA

JOHN HUNT PUBLISHING

First published by Moon Books, 2021
Moon Books is an imprint of John Hunt Publishing Ltd., No. 3 East Street, Alresford
Hampshire SO24 9EE, UK
office@jhpbooks.net
www.johnhuntpublishing.com
www.moon-books.net

For distributor details and how to order please visit the 'Ordering' section on our website.

Text copyright: David Sparenberg 2021

ISBN: 978 1 78904 973 2
978 1 78904 974 9 (ebook)
Library of Congress Control Number: 2021938954

Design: Matthew Greenfield

UK: Printed and bound by CPI Group (UK) Ltd, Croydon, CR0 4YY
Printed in North America by CPI GPS partners

Published in association Pagan Dawn, a Pagan Federation magazine.

We operate a distinctive and ethical publishing philosophy in
all areas of our business, from our global network of authors to
production and worldwide distribution.

Contents

...the rule of no realm is mine...great or small. But all worthy things that are in peril as the world now stands, those are my care. And for my part, I shall not wholly fail of my task...
if anything passes through the night that can still grow fair or bear fruit and flower...
For I also am a steward. Did you not know?
Gandalf, from Return of the King - J.R.R. Tolkien

To each and all of my kindred where we meet heart to heart and soul to soul: I, in the sear of life, greet you in dialogue and the springtime promise of renewal:

To all who align yourselves with Great Spirit, Creator of Heaven and Earth, dedicated to the maintenance of life;

To all who are Rainbow Warriors of Love, who love tenderly where tenderness is welcomed, who love fiercely where fierce love is needed;

To all Warriors of Spirit, who maintain honesty, integrity, and who fight for the prevalence of truth over lies and corruption and violence. Those of you who dedicate your lives to planting seeds in the sub-culture fertility of soul and the accepting hearts of children, convinced that a time is coming when forests of light will flourish globally, and there will be peace, and with peace awareness and justice.

To you, sisters (ascending into power), brothers (steadfast in support), children of goodness and good friends, this dedication to healing the abused Earth, to a human return to dialogic belonging and to sanity, and to the openness and welcoming back maturely among us, after misdirection, misdeeds and exile, the Spirit of Beauty, of Light and Balance, and of Life:

I, in the sear of my time, dedicate this invitation to you.

Essays

Confronting Crisis and the
Specter of Critical Mass

Albert Camus wrote something along these lines: "We need to stop making war on one another and unite against the common enemies of humanity – disease, poverty, death". The global pandemic is a challenge for nations and individuals alike. We live on a Trauma Planet and the COVID-19 crisis is not the only crisis coming our way. There are lessons to be learned if we will learn them. Tragically Camus' humanitarian appeal has been ignored so far. But here we are, daily facing questions of the value of life and decisions will be made from the experience we are all sharing, decisions about the future of Earth and Humanity. Not one without the other, not one in disregard or at the exclusion of the other. Questions: Who will be the decision makers? Who will leave the responsibility to others? These are not new questions of course. Ortega Y Gasset raised the same in his classic study *The Revolt of the Masses* in the era of rising Fascism in Spain and across Europe. The questions do however take on new relevance and an increased burden of critical responsibility.

To choose to get over our now-crisis and forget it is to choose to perpetuate the history of suffering and calamity. In the other direction, if we will learn, truly learn, from the lessons behind fear and selfish carelessness, for us there can emerge new opportunities to define common ground and common goals. Can you imagine, someday looking over your shoulder at the backward of time and realizing you were part of human unity, a participant in the process of renewal and sanity and, yes, even peace? And why? Because the work at hand was (or is) given priority over the forces of destruction.

The suffering, hardships, anxieties, sacrifices and the losses are real, will continue and increase. But is it so bad to slow down, to practice quiet, to be at home and to come to value life and the lives of others above the false security of things and profit? We live on this planet. Life on Earth addresses us. Now, what are we being told to do (it is not hard to decipher), but to make changes, first in behaviors and habitual patterns, beyond that, to change how we identify ourselves, individually, in statehood, and as a species, and how we connect.

Not without clear recognition and not without compassion, I feel the need to ask: What are we willing and able to learn and who and how are we willing and able to be when again we are released to reenter the social world? We may not make it, and some of us certainly will not, to where we should be arriving. But in unity and direction we might possibly participate in a renaissance of relationships. This will depend in part on how we think and how we feel, what systems we sustain and what systems change or dismantle, or whether we collectively emerge with a spirit of humility to guide us, instead of broken habits and arrogance driving us as we push Earth ever further into the meta-historical abyss of our suicidal madness.

To speak of this is not to sound a happy note. To the contrary. It is what former American vice president Al Gore has called "An Inconvenient Truth." Both sides of this designation are significant. The traumatic condition of Gaia-Earth is inconvenient for humanity and more than inconvenient, threatening to the normalcy of secular, self-referential modern civilization. And it is true to reality and to necessity and therefore is truth insofar as we, Earth born, Earth dwelling, bearers of conscious mortality, are evolved to comprehend what truth is.

Here is an important point of distinction I shall make at the onset. We are not yet at critical mass in terms of potentially being overwhelmed by eco and geo cataclysm. But are well on our way to it being unprecedented. Where we are is on a threshold, at a crossroads where decisions are being made to determine direction. Understand this clearly. I am not an alarmist. I do not welcome dead zones covering land and sea or nonstop environmental terror-episodes consuming populations. But I am joined by multitudes who know alarms sounding. An existential threat is ominously near and the event horizon of cataclysmic critical mass comes into view.

What do I mean though by critical mass? It is what the scientific community begins to talk about as "the point of no return." How can it happen that we, meaning our species aggressively compelling much else if not all of life on Earth, to a "point of no return", meaning conditions so adverse that life cannot be within safety, sanity, or dignity? A point beyond which life may not be possible.

I have already sided with Camus in appealing for decency and affirming the value of life, and not life as an abstraction, but individual lives, concrete collective lives, even relational interspecies lives. I have chosen not to carelessly stir up dystopian dread. At the same time, I have committed myself to paying attention to the world clock, noting that the hour of the planet is late, and to awaken others to the magnitude of horrific troubles fomenting around us.

Allow me then to outline two types of what I intend by our reaching planetary critical mass. The first critical mass would be this: The number and intensity of ecological or geological catastrophes occur within an approximate time frame and geo-physical region exceeding the capability of human systems to adequately respond and recover. This would apply to incapacitating already poor communities and countries with shallow resources as well as their wealthy neighbors and nations where resources are deep yet still proving inadequate. The second condition of critical mass would be triggered by a cataclysmic environmental event (better if we designate such happening as a totalizing anti-event). For example, we might consider the scientific theory that the impact of a massive meteor brought about the extinction of dinosaurs or dare to think the so-called unthinkable and speculate on how total thermonuclear war would eliminate life and any future possibility of life. Again, an entrance into critical mass could be through a permanent weather pattern shift moved in magnitude from catastrophe to catastrophe to outright global cataclysm and, once more, exceeding every possibility of recuperative response. All of this is to say that Earth can be pushed to the point of no return by human inappropriateness, to suddenly overwhelm humanity, ending human domination, obliterating civilization, and concluding in the extinction of ourselves and most other planetary species. While there remains time (and not much remains) why do we keep "progressing" toward the brink, trekking on unto endgame, compulsively toward the manmade light out of apocalypse?

If our embrace of life and the gratuitous justice of habitation of each in its kind is stronger than any romanticized attraction to death or religious expectation, we can change ourselves and our choices, our collective values, and our collective direction. Critical mass approaches (and we are driving the speeding vehicle) and we, in our contemporary generations are reaching the determining threshold. Critical mass approaches and we, in delusion, inertia, procrastination or else with purposive solidarity, are at our future defining crossroads. The biggest, if not ultimate, questions for us are where are we headed and why and where do we intend the future to be? On a habitable planet or in a lifeless blackhole?

Because I am not an alarmist but only one of many who knows alarms are sounding – out of Greenland, from the Polar Vortex, across the Sahara, the Amazon and on and on – I will, counterintuitively, close on a note of hope. Not fictive hope, but hope grounded in reality-and-necessity, and with deep trust in the spiritually empowering essence of humanity.

I mention Greta Thunberg, the movement she has become the face of, and all the millions of world youth who are inspired in their conscience to join Greta in demanding of powerbrokers alternatives guaranteeing a habitable Earth for succeeding generations with governance of sufficiency, stability, and dignity. Every one of us should be grateful to those who demand through courageous, nonviolent assertions a tomorrow of positive possibilities free of the dread of impending ecological apocalypse; they, being honest enough in their hour to confront crisis as it is, ready and willing to stand for the changes necessary becoming universally normative.

Camus was one of the last outstanding humanitarians and his influence continues to reach across time. It has been more than fifty years since a chorus of voices began to be raised, signaling the need for addressing the future state of the planet. There have been many integral, outstanding voices drawing attention to the converging storm of environmental and human crisis. Some of the living have heeded the calls and warnings and some have not, falsifying the summons and dismissing it. I come in the latter-day status of a distinguished tradition, the long lines of Earth attentive advocates, activists, eco-prophets, and shaman-pathfinders. My contribution is not to add to the existing abundance of information on what is going wrong and what should be done to correct it. My strength and intentions are to shine a few rays of ennobling light into dark recesses of anguish, hopelessness, despair. Perhaps to awaken some souls to spiritual healing and the work of mending Earth while bettering our disillusioned, delusional, endangered, traumatically damaged, and endangering species. I am convinced that humanity is a traumatized species responsible for inflicting trauma, in consequence, on the living Earth and Earth's diversity of inhabitants, because we carry through generations the fragmentations and untreated wounds of historical atrocities – wars of death and destruction against our kind and this accelerating war waged by mankind against all realms of nature, from which we are alienated, toward which we are hardened in cruelty and indifference. I will insist that we are spiritually better than history finds us. We are not only "thrown" into the world, we are also capable of rising above circumstances and being responsible for the world. We can believe in the power of the moral voice, the vulnerable look, of the compassionate heart and soul of love. We can make such beliefs into Earth Spirituality and such spirituality foundational,

My personal wish for Earth and the continuance of Gaia's evolutionary diversity is that we humans work our way to maturity, that one day, and not as a wish upon a distant star, we collectively emerge, that is evolve, into Avatars of Relationships. We can, like creation itself, always at a point of genesis, forever beginning, diurnally renewing, move in that direction. It is not that this going to be easy. It will not be easy. But we are not here for comfort and convenience, consuming everything, soiling the nest, trashing the elements, leaving dead zones in our wake, and an exhausted and vengeful Earth in a fury of death throes. I am not convinced to give up, I tenaciously refuse to abandon trust, even against the odds, in still unrealized possibilities of spiritually evolving humanity.

No evasions, henceforth, no more excuses or self-serving denials. Let us rather see; as honest women and men, as parent and grandparents, friends, loved ones, neighbors; what great work is to be done to confront the crisis of our making and prevail from crisis to justice and out of the reckoning of justice to attempt healing. It was the Medieval Swiss physician, alchemist, and natural philosopher, Paracelsus, who said that within every disease are the terms of cure and a way to the restoration of health.

The admonition of Camus, as initially stated, has not yet been heeded. Do I believe that my voice will be more effective than his? Not at all. But neither will I give up on the voice of conscience prevailing in the depths of peoples.

A Clarifying Note on the
Magnitude of Earth Crisis

Much of my creative work these days (and indeed for decades before) is to address the mounting and sometimes engulfing Earth Crisis within which we are all entangled, which threatens us daily and overshadows the future.

Earth Crisis is not only Climate Change, although climate change is a major component of Earth Crisis. Other components of the ongoing global condition confronting and challenging life, include rampant pollution and toxicity of land, atmosphere and waters (with oceans in particular being negatively impacted by flotillas of plastic, so many floating necropolises over dead zones), ever accelerating depletion of natural resources, the reduction of diverse species habitation, massive extinctions of species causing proliferating regional collapses of eco-systems, and the seldom evaluated and more seldomly articulated ecology of war. It is generally overlooked that modern war technology is environment altering and poisoning technology, with broad, long term consequences for botanic and biotic diversity, and human health.

Climate change, which is visibly impacting millions and gaining popular recognition and political traction in most nations, is important to accept and act on. At the same time, climate change, as a known term for events of pressing endangerment, can also provide a perspective of focus and a vital starting point for changing human assumptions and behaviors contra the fuller dynamics of Earth Crisis. Every component touched on here is interwoven with every other. When we address one, we, whether reluctantly or willingly, discover how it is part of the rest.

Ultimately, there is no way to acknowledge and respond to Earth Crisis in a sustainable, holistic manner without accepting that Earth Crisis is Human Crisis.

This planet has evolved as the known place of life, as habitat for diversity, as home ground. What is happening to the planet is not apart from us, although we are but a singular, while co-inhabiting, species-part of all that lives here. Directly, it is happening with and from and through us – the currently dominating, ubiquity of the human. Along with Earth being brought to trial by human intervention and impact, our humanity is simultaneously brought to trial.

The presence of the human is yet another (no doubt for us most significant), component of Earth Crisis. While we work with united dedication to correct the course of climate change, we need to inquire and take upon ourselves with equal dedication what the terms of identity, history, social organization, economic systems, and patterns of consumption and necessity, have been and are, and why.

How can there be a sustainable solution that is partial when the problem involves the organic whole, made up of vital relationships and interdependencies, and the whole of the problem is being directly driven, and thereby will be determined, by our planetary presence? We exist here among shrinking otherness and collectively are the cause behind species and systems imbalances. Yet collectively we are far from being sufficiently accountable for the extremes of human negatives – exploitation, disruption, misuse and overuse – and the already occurring and potential consequences.

Earth Crisis is Earth Changes. Earth Changes involve traumas, transformations and sacrifices. We too, an Earth species, must change, not with increased aggressiveness and not in bitterness, but with an Ecosophy, an Earth Wisdom of the reverence and dedication to the protection of life. Earth is a Life Place. Why do we choose existence in a so-called civilization threatening Earth with upheavals, waste, and desolation?

Within the ongoing Earth Crisis, time is not on our side

and species wide we are already called to an international mobilization of moral character and courage, and an immediate, intergenerational cultivation of response-ability as disaster preparedness and survival education. We need ask: What terms of a future await life if we continue to pretend and deny? What terms of Earth future if we change course and sustain proliferating facets of alternatives? If we unite in disciplined dedication to making of the Age of Extinctions an Ecozoic Era*?

*The words Ecosophy (eco-philosophy) and Ecosopher (eco-philosopher) originated with the Norwegian philosopher Arnie Naess. The word Ecosophy has come to replace Deep Ecology. The term Ecozoic Era (an age of eco-responsibility to counter the current age of extinctions) was coined by Thomas Berry.

Looking

One of the true lessons I learned from RD Laing was to observe each person and entity from more than one perspective. Life is dynamic and in one sense or another every encounter is in process, and how we approach a presence initiates openness and response. The more fully we observe the more we become aware of, and the less likely to be narrow minded and make snap judgments based on self-absorption, preconception, and a one-dimensional point of view. The less inclined, in truth, to decide to ignore or to deny this someone or something of encounter based on subjectivity and internal monologue. We are one with our bodies, yes, body proud and ego-bound, yet we are inclined to openness. We are skintight, yes, yet we are relatable out of porousness.

To change perspective is to extend duration, intensify focus and to recognize the ambiguity inherent in all human encounters. Who or what is this we are seeing? Who or what the presence we now meet? Changing perspective is motion. It moves duration and distance and details. By extending engagement and diversifying points of view, the observer too is taken into a process of mutuality. Mutuality applies to interpersonal relationships, artistic endeavors, and, importantly, as well, to ecology. Dialogue that arrives in mutuality, in a place of encounter, makes possible a closeup view.

The French Impressionist painter Paul Cezanne for a time in his last years lived in Provence where he observed, approached, and painted from various vantage points through seasons Mount Sainte-Victoire, artistically questing to capture in this serial concentration a moment in the essence of the mountain. A mountain, of course, is not necessary to enter here, to become engaged or creatively absorbed. The same is open to happening on any, including a small, scale. But to maintain the reference to

Cezanne we might consider how the points of view of Sainte-Victoire changed in the visioning of the painter and the acts of painting how he was seeing the mountain made changes in the identity of the artist. Regardless of medium, a process of spiraling amplifications sets to work with life altering residual effect. The painter is in part his paintings, the musician in part his music, the dancer her dancing, the actress her acting, the poet his or her poetry. Is there a level outside of ordinary consciousness where Cezanne's mountain is also subject to change? Multiplicity emerges in this and unity, as gathering, becomes integral out of interweaving multiplicity. We might call such the patterns of interlacement.

Laing once made a training video to show us how differing points of view of a single subject yield differing perceptions and a subject that was mundane becomes mystical, that was beautiful becomes grotesque; the one and same being brilliant becomes lackluster and vice versa, and the apparently dull is otherwise experienced to conceal a subtle secret, a buried vitality, scintillation, fascination, and affinity.

To draw close to recognition and participation experiences unity as a skein, a multiplicity of homeostatic and antithetical images and impressions and requires patience. Perhaps also an effective interplay of humility and courage. We do not, however, inhabit a patient world. Unity of humility and courage are rarely found together in advanced industrial and cybernetic societies.

How often, then; denying ourselves and our sense of being relationally-with and belonging-to; do we hurry by the meeting-of-otherness and with-otherness and miss thereby what will not happen for us without us? Who and whatever we do not look at, we do not see. Who and what we do not dare to linger before, when the possibility of connection presents itself, flattens existence, threatens to deaden vitality, and pass over the wondrous intricacies of natural diversity. Porousness is replaced by cracks. One is to be spontaneously receptive (porous), while the other (cracks) be exactly what it implies, "cracked up," fragmented. Cracks contribute nothingness, the vacancy of falling apart, and then into the abyss of psychosis and history.

Through the time of our lives, we are choosing between bitterness and innocence, between walls and openness, between joyous participation and the angst of isolation; exclusion of dimensions and points of view, or looking as the risk taking of adventure; the sensory and concrete attempts at a mutuality of dialogue with that which comes out before us, confronts, with surprise, force or quiet grace, and is relational. As badly as we must relearn to sing the world, we must also and with increasing urgency, be reeducated in looking; caring for what our attracted senses communicate; and connecting.

Illusion or Presence

A friend who lives but a short distance from Tara Hill, home of the ancient High Kings of Ireland, writes to me saying, "It is all an illusion, isn't it?" The remark is a question. A genuine question is hunger and a form of waiting. A question may not wait for an answer, but it inevitably waits for a response. Here is mine.

As I am no more in the God-position than yourself, I cannot make the pronouncement that "All" is an illusion. From my life within the truth of this Living Earth, I do not find it so.

A tree for me is not an illusion. A tree is a presence. It has its own laws. A tree abides in its tree-ness, in its tree reality. Also, every tree has a context making life possible. The question I ask myself is what is the nature of my response to the presence of the tree? Is my response an act of beauty, a way of singing the world of this tree-particular? Or is it a reduction of tree presence to an object to be viewed or ignored, used, or eventually destroyed?

Is the child you love and care for an illusion or a presence? An alive entity growing according to the condition of human life and the laws of human growth woven into the laws of nature? Is the child an emergent potential within the dynamic field of existence, or is the child merely an illusion? Or worse yet, is the child or any child a possession?

What of creatures, in the nonhuman or transhuman realm, shall we say sheep grazing on a countryside hill in the green of spring? I see them in my inevitably particular way, yet I am also capable of recognizing that they, sheep, are a form of living otherness, with sheep realities which yet, somehow in the evolutionary unfolding of biotic diversity, for both sheep and I, are relational.

With tree, with child, with sheep, relationships are possible by accepting each reality as a presence, a life form beyond but touching upon myself, my self-awareness, my living self as also a presence. This is astonishing to me! Nor would I exchange my astonishment for a view of the Great Cosmic Mandala, the Maya-web of speculation should I, in the exchange, lose my focus of the earthen sensuality and perceptivity wherein I exist.

My friend in writing uses the word "interpretation" several times, apparently to demonstrate the relative value of illusions. But I take it differently.

Interpretations, certainly! Being interpreters – interpreters and surveyors – is a signature-value of who we are as species humanity and may well come to be recognized as a primary function of our collective evolution and biotic community worth.

Interpretations can be contrived and made convoluted to deliberately obscure; to miss the mark, be a smoke and mirrors trick, cunningly beside the point, covertly promoting an intention, cause, or purpose other than genuine contact and the exploring through dialogue of mutually accepted terms (exchanges) of truth and reality. This we might call the dark side, or at least prelude to the dark side, where shadows lengthen in distrust, disappointment, bitterness, and betrayal. Yet on the sunny side, where shadows are shortened by the prevalence of light, interpretations can be entrances into dialogues of adventure, risk, connectivity, and to arriving "in" the mutuality of recognition which is also a presence interfacing presence (or person with person) entering onto a shared ground of openness and potentially embrace in respect or even reverence.

Facilitating interpretation of the genuine dialogic process (subjective evaluation extending outward, "out toward," as welcome and invitation) begins with what we observe and experience, and the growth transformation of what we need and what we desire from another presence or another person. In the process it is important to remember that there is a world of difference (and I mean this quite literally) between manipulation of thingness and encounter – between the illusions of imposition, use or domination, and the open event of meeting.

Far too often, especially in cluttered and deception rewarding societies, things dominate identities, individuals, and masses pell-mell habitually place their own intentions, schemes. and desires between openness and other. Unfortunately, illusion then and illusion-making takes over, and illusions can come to hide, distort, or negate the reality of presence. This too is of the dark side, traffics in control, and is a form of slavery and abnegation.

Clarifying self-knowledge is an invaluable platform from which to initiate the process of maturation into living "within" truth of the Living Earth, and into the truths of relationship possibilities. From self-knowledge arises values – honesty, reverence, respect, courage and humility, integrity, and best of all seeing well and seeing with the eyes of your soul. Soul is deep seeing. Allowed, soul is attuned. Soul is depth in nature. And soul is power.

Starting from Blake

Here I am about to share a few reflections on a quotation from William Blake. I came across the Blake while recently rereading, in *Per Amica Silentia Lunea*, the *Anima Mundi* by WB Yeats. Here is Blake's single line:

"God only acts or is in existing beings and men."

These few words put a fire in my head. Out of associations with this small quotation emerges a pattern of thought I am moved to share. Quickly I step beyond the commonplace response: "Ah, here is another confirmation that we are God!" My mind turns in a different direction.

Thus: Every act of violence destroying life out of season, whether human or otherwise – violence as cold will or cruelty – causes imbalance, diminishing the Presence of God in this specialized, variegated yet thoroughly interwoven world we inhabit, abuse, and interdependently share.

When this old Earth is soaked in the blood of injustice, disrespect, disregard and oppression, God (or, if your belief prefers, Goddess) is exiled. The exile is infinite and eternal suffering. The deeper the wound, the darker the curse, the further and further removal becomes in convoluting losses of betrayal and distrust.

I wish to impress the seriousness of divine affliction and the twofold consequences of divine exile. Because, if you are honest in your humanity, this will cause heartache and heartbreak. And a broken heart can be the beginning of redirecting and redefining change.

What then, a person asks, can be the possible terms to end and reverse this exile, and for return of the Presence of the numinous, Holy, of Goddess-God as an opening way of eventful encounter between us? Between the Holy and being human.

The mystic will imagine the content of two genuine possibilities for this ultimate event: the terror – the terror of all conceivable terrors – of all consuming and purging conflagration or holocaust of eradicating fire; or a sustainable cultivation of Heaven on Earth by non-exclusionary, encompassing love. Annihilation or ardent compassion. Extinction or a stewardship of sustainable biotic justice.

On one side is the zeitgeist of endgame, a solution we have collectively permitted and even prepared for ourselves. On the opposite horizon is suggested the evolutionary maturity of the divine-human dialogue.

Always the living need to choose and choose often, choosing between the degrees of death, our inherited demons, and the deeper inner whisperings of the affirmations of life, our too long neglected and too often forgotten species ancestry: between consumption in cataclysmic or apocalyptic horror, or deliverance through enlightening peace; between destruction, which we have nearly perfected, and creaturely love, which we are at risk of losing the warmth and light of through technology, and even forsaking the spontaneity of natural and native (non-exploitative) feeling for.

What is most difficult, difficult to the extent of being dangerous in the contemporary condition, is the accelerating and pandemic problematic of history, moving, without sufficiently empowered critical resistance, toward the negative conclusion – a finalizing event (or should we identify anti-event?) of the human adventure (or must we say misadventure?). The while, soul retrieval (and with the exile of God, or Goddess, as Presence declines the visionary clarity of soul and with eclipsing of soul's revelatory perception comes the extensive exiling of soul), retrieval then, awakening, empowering liberation, setting in motion the cultivation of response-ability – all of this takes place on a different scale from the thrust of history; unfolds in biorhythms of necessity, at a slower (should I not name it?), saner pace. The threat of annihilation being linear, the alternative made up of correspondences and connections is, within the matrix of Goddess-God and nature, recurrently circular and episodic.

Time has ever been and urgently, if not menacingly, continues to be the arbiter of Earth's phases and direction.

Now this bundle of thoughts initiates another quotation. Perhaps it is all but an exercise in the associative peculiarity of personal thinking? Be that as it may, since I started out on a small quotation from Blake, it feels somewhat appropriate to conclude on another. This is from the French author and philosopher Albert Camus.

The sensitive reader will follow the curve of this association, especially in knowing that I end with these words because I am in stubborn agreement with them. Here is Camus:

"This is perhaps what I felt most deeply. At every form that miscarries in the trenches, at every outline, metaphor or prayer crushed under steel, the eternal loses a round. Conscious that I cannot stand aloof from my time, I have decided to be an integral part of it." *

The problematic is the question mark and presence of humanity. The crisis is humanity, having spilled over, through technology and organized violence, into Earth crisis and through arrogance, resentment and isolating self-reference, into our species withdrawal from and abnegation of former forms of divine-human dialogue. History is the consuming abyss, become an existential threat. These times are our challenge and are what they are. Camus chose against suicide and murder, between reason and hell. Now **we** are the choosing ones.

from The Myth of Sisyphus: Conquest

Warriors of Ancestral Plain*

An autumn morning: I had been out across the river, walking in the fields. A small poem came into me. I repeated the words several times aloud, committing them to memory.

When I returned home, however, I was not convinced the poem should be written down. I thought its content was perhaps picked up from reading Yeats or Goethe's Faust. Uncertain, I stood before the fireplace debating in my mind, while gazing up at a portrait of Beethoven.

Suddenly I felt I was no longer alone; rather, I was being watched from behind. The feeling had that same uncanny sharpness that comes upon us when we sense that somebody unseen has their eyes on us.

Turning around I was surprised – not startled or frightened, but quietly surprised – at seeing a group of gentle, distinguished souls of various ages who were crowding into the room. They stood looking at me and many of them, especially those who were nearest, stood smiling. And thus, without a word spoken, the bright ones collectively communicated with me: "Yes, write it down. That poem is true. It is our truth for sharing." Upon this, the benevolent souls gathered before me faded away.

That was more than forty years ago. The episode of encounter behind the mere poem's coming on is more profound than the poem itself. Not of the message of the poem but the small, poor words with which I clothe it. Still here it is, with some slight revisions including a title change.

The original title was *Communion*, for to me that is what took place. I have retitled it now *Warriors of the Ancestral Plain*. This is my present interpretation of the poem stimulated visitation.

Here it is:

> Every time we rename a name
> Every time we remember a face
> You, bright kindred of the crossing place
> Warriors
> Of Ancestral Plain
> Live once more
> In our intensity.
>
> Sun awakening
> Sweet Mother Earth.
> Mystery clouds
> In dreams of light!
> I sing to you:
> Earth Faithful Ones.
>
> To all who lived with life's true face
> To all who lived in love's embrace
> To all who live
> With love and grace
> (Gentle and courageous souls):
> I sing to you.

In these latter days I think this early poem is not only telling of what is to come, what can come next, but of how to live here, so to get from any here to there in the wisdom of my visitors; some whose passion for life was not extinguished even by death; and how there is a bond between the life we have now and the life of the journey hereafter. Reality is porous. That is a statement deserving much serious reflection.

Clarity and openness – receive-ability and response-ability – everyday dignity and heroic joy are high values in dimensions where truth folds and unfolds without a sense of time, yet with diverse, co-creative rhythms, patterns. The Warriors of the Ancestral Plain are steadfast ones who have trusted once and gone on to strive thereafter in the pathfinding wisdom of the soul: in love, that ever promises a heroic dawn opening beyond night's narrow passage through death.

*The Earth-Spirit Warriors written of here are from among those fierce and tender lovers and artists of human ancestry who lived their lives of passionate intensity in fearlessness (courage) and gentleness (compassion and humility). In the pathos of lived belonging, they have not sought release to venture on into other worlds but stay attentive to the joys and sorrows, the crimes, follies, and celebrations of life in this spherical place of mothering power. They, bygone Earth-Spirit Warriors, are the once embodied who continue ethereally among us. Mostly they remain silent. Mostly they are invisible. But their language, made not of words but emotions, is eloquent and their revelations portentous.

Parzival in a Nutshell

Eventually it was revealed that under the magnificent armor of the Red Knight, Parzival remained in the clothes of a pagan fool, even as his mother had dressed him when he first rode from his wild wood home into the world. Observing mockingly, an attendant queen said to the young warrior, "You are crazy!" "How should I not be both fool and crazy?" Parzival replied. "I am the one who failed to ask the question of questions and my suffering in consequence shall be a long ordeal."

If at first meeting, Parzival had asked the Fisher King, "What ails you?' the royal fisherman would have answered, "I have a wound. The wound has crippled me. It is the nature of this crippling that has left me impotent. From my impotence the land is desolation, not garden – the land is waste." But to have asked without the quest of years would have, of course, been astonishment, a superhuman achievement. Parzival needed to embrace his human vulnerability and the beauty and limitations of conscious mortality.

Over time it was Parzival who would come to highest honor at Arthur's Round Table, who would ask at last the question and heal the wound of the Fisher King, who would dispel the curse, returning the Waste Land to abundant life, and would himself, with quest fulfilled, become a Keeper of the Grail Castle. Therein to celebrate the Grail Herself. That was astonishment, only out of what Kierkegaard called the "wound of possibility." As the spiritual condition of King and Land are one, so too the mystic eros of the Grail Maiden and the Holy Grail.

This is my brief synopsis of the epic poem *Parzival* by Wolfram von Eschenback. Those who are initiated into the teachings of Alchemy – the union of opposites, the philosopher's stone, the elixir – whether directly from manuscripts or through the depth psychology interpretations of Jung, Von Franz, and others, will

24

find it easy enough to read between the lines and flush out the story of this Medieval Romance, thereby putting into place the missing puzzle pieces. To those not familiar, in delight I recommend two helpful readings. First is the groundbreaking classic *From Ritual to Romance* by Jessie Weston. The other, more contemporary, being a collection of Joseph Campbell's posthumous essays on the subject: *Romance of the Grail - Magic and Mystery of Arthurian Myth*. Regardless of your approach to the individualization process, I admonish you to toss from your memory all references to Wagner.

True, Parzival comes from the wild woods to Arthur's court in Avalon, but not via Bayreuth. Parzival learns that force is not an answer. Domination is not an answer, dogma, no answer. Through his maturation the hero comes to embrace the awakening that the pagan innocence of the fool abides behind the psychic armor of conquest, that the beauty and sentient vulnerability of the face lives longingly behind the rigid masks of civilizational ideologies.

Blessing Way and Prayer to the Interior Forms of the Earth

The Navajo (Dineh) people of the American southwest practice sacred ceremonies and prayers of Hozho (Blessing) to renew the order of creation: confirm or reset the proper relationships between human communities and the other-than-human communities of our natural biosphere. This is the Blessing Way, the way of respect, appropriate alignment, of coming into, or returning to, original at-onement. Within the elaborate Blessing Way Ceremony humans are not viewed or treated as a breed apart, but are significant participants in intricate, inter-related and interdependent, global, even cosmic, eco-systems. Within this vast dynamic, sometimes called the Sacred Hoop of Creation, humans have a specific role, the role of embodying, articulating, memorializing, prayers of time-space renewals and ceremonies reenacting primordial appropriation (role and placement) and resulting harmony.

Within the Blessing Way is the prayer called the Navajo Prayer of the Internal Forms of the Earth, the shortened title of which is simply Earth Prayer. A visionary sensibility is required to be able to "know;" to be relational, even intimate, with the interior (spiritual) forms, present everywhere, of diverse, living Earth entities.

Within the heritage wisdom of Navajo (Dineh) traditionalists and ceremonialists, Hozho (Blessing) is synonymous "with proper order." This says, "There is a way for everything, and that way is blessed as it was decreed in sacred history." How does this apply in the here and now and to the present disorder and disconnected and imperialistic structuring of the modern human world? The politics of a lifestyle exceed the general definitions of politics and are manifested in the politics of experience and worldview.

Before the current, pandemic crisis mandating human

withdrawal into non-action, minimizing and quieting mainstream behaviors, the other-than-human species and compositional materials of the Earth flourish and begin to reposition. It is spring and we can witness, from our circumscribed invasiveness, spring's diversity coming forth, unfolding in spaces we had recently dominated. Trees' blossom, flowers emerge, the numbers and varieties of birds increase; we can watch and listen to these autonomous changes. Dolphins are reported swimming the canals of Venice! Deer casually wander through traffic free suburban streets! Curious sheep stand idly on uncropped British lawns!

The examples are powerful addresses. They provide meaningful lessons. Look into a mirror. Look into the eyes of the person nearest you. Ask: what are you learning? There are vaster resources in the right questions being asked at the right time, than in the presumptions of expedient answers. The audacity, the daring, of the Socratic method of examining the who and what and wherefore of personal and civic life! In the Blessing Way humans relive the miracles of creation. In the chaos of illusions lessons are not learned.

In the Blessing Way Ceremony is a chant including these lines:

"Before Earth with the small blue birds it is blessed/with small blue birds around me it is blessed as I say this."

The chant closes with the direct action of vital, participatory expression. Here is a reflection from ecologists Peter Knudtson and David Suzuki:

"The Navajo prayers of the Earth reveal a profound empathy for nature and its various forms, even an ecstatic identity with a religious veneration for them. These very qualities would be essential to any meaningful science-compatible ceremonies of world renewal that Western societies may, by urgent necessity, be compelled to create within the decades ahead." *

27

I will extract key words and phrases from this statement, inviting to a deep contemplation upon which to meditate. Such are these: *empathy, ecstatic identity, veneration, essential, ceremonies of world renewal, urgent necessity, compelled to create, in decades ahead.* Let me next construct a comprehensive sentence from these words and phrases to focus experiential-attention on the lesson we could and should be learning: *Empathy, ecstatic identity, veneration* (integrated into) *essential ceremonies of world renewal* (are) *urgently necessary* (enactments we will be) *compelled to create in the decades ahead.* That is, I add: If we, the wayward, startled and baffled along the evolutionary continuum, are to endure, even to survive within affirming, habitable conditions; planetary conditions; of biotic justice, directional sanity, systemic renewal and sustainable (bio-regionally sensitive) ecosophy. If we would return, I am suggesting, to the sacred, recover the Blessing Way, live our lives together as flesh and body-soul of Earth Prayer, we are bound to take cues from sources such as Navajo ceremonial wisdom, creating reality -based teachings, rituals, and stories to validate sensibilities of the human right to continue, as belonging beings not devouring invaders. Will challenges generate an increase in blind arrogance, greed, and aggression; truly the traits of being a breed apart; or instill a sufficiency of humility to make future habitation a qualitative possibility?

It is only, I believe, in the cultivation of responsibility as an intergenerational ability to respond to what is real and what necessary for the conditions of this planet and to do what is biotically right for life that the human species arrives in a state of clarity, disciple and dedication that amounts to an actuality of what enlightenment and maturity are purposely to be in this time of trial and trauma.

Wisdom of Elders by Peter Knudtson & David Suzuki

The Next Phase

The process of individualization is the current phase of human evolution. This phase began to democratize at the European Renaissance. Now it wanes. The two World Wars increased the scale of human targeting – in state terrorism, suffering and annihilation. Auschwitz was the terminus of civilization; the atomic atrocities of Hiroshima, Nagasaki, warnings against omnicide. The largess of human personality vanishes. Environmental consequences of modern warfare are scarcely spoken of. We continue in systems of falsification and exploitation and a culture of extravagance and violence. What is wordless is unthinkable. When naming happens the named is open to endless communication.

The next phase of human evolution is the transformation of ego-self into eco-self. In core dynamics this shift involves turning the long journey into the interior outward to geo-biotic relationships and in dialectic alternations between reaching deeply into the past of origins and moving conditionally into an Ecozoic Future*.

In the ongoing century this, which is already an affinitive calling, will democratize further. The coming on of this spreading and taking root; more and more comprehensively reshaping contours and the content of existence; opens the greater possibilities of human survival, sanity, and planetary stability.

Likely this will democratize only out of increasing and intensifying tragedies, reducing global human presence to sustainable levels. Challenges are unprecedented. The process into eco-self-identity and Earth-based affirmation is terrifying, winnowing, yet sublime.

Persons dedicated to the next phase should willingly support one another, learning and mastering living between tragedy and necessity. Each should serve as an invitation to directional dialogue. Alert senses, emotional spontaneity, intuition, and critical thinking – with the goal of mature response-ability – are vital powers in the shaping of the Practical Gestalten of an Ecozoic Era.

Only in the presence of a life-altering event (or in response to a traumatic, life-altering anti-event) does integrity fully manifest and define human identity. The fulfilment of spiritual evolution for this time of crisis is in the passionate affirmation of life across the entire biotic spectrum as against the hopelessness, indifference, and enervating trivialization of the human condition in an obscenity of species detachment, isolation, values falsification.

It is in the ascension of the next phase for pathfinders in quest of new directions to apply the Native American attitude of doing what is done with a signature of identity for seven generations, each generation working for yet seven more to follow thereafter. Even if it dreams over the rainbow, as practicum of the next phase, the Great Work plans both now and beyond the horizon for a condition of welcoming, in health and wellbeing, by those now present for the sake of others unborn.

Aggression, cruelty, arrogance, malignance, and greed are among the worst human traits. Tenacity and tenderness, kindness, humility, courage, companionship, and the openness to participate with creation in reverence and respect give countenance to the best of who and what we can be. The greater benevolence of human beings is yet to become. We begin by welcoming receptivity to our senses and turning love outward to the realities and needs of the Living Earth as our one-only sustaining home. We evolute into being at home by practicing the Beauty Way – in relearning the ancestral art of relationships.

To harden is to become a mask – not the protective mask against pandemic but the iron mask of self-referential and interpersonal incarcerations. That mask is moribund and belongs to death. To be familied into the next phase of human evolution is to be mutually vulnerable, porous, and thus be on the way to becoming authenticated as Ecosophers of the Ecozoic. Why not call this transition salvation? Why not name this pursuit heroic? Why not mandate that the embracing of life (Human and Holy) is sacred? That the real work of humanity on this Earth is to participate in keeping Earth habitable, healthy, beautiful through acts of beauty – through doing what is right for life to do: why not?

*Again, the terms Ecosophy and Ecosopher were coined by the Norwegian philosopher Arne Ness to substitute for Deep Ecology. Ecozoic (and Ecozoic Era) come from geo-theological Thomas Berry, author of The Great Work and The Dream of the Earth.

Majority Report

There is something at the very core about us that needs to change. This cannot be emphasized often enough. We need to change how we think. How we think of ourselves, our place in creation, how we think of how we live, how we think of our relationships to the diversity of planetary life, to structures, elements, systems of nature and interconnections of naturally functioning Earth ways.

To change how we think do we first change the normalcy of perception? Or does perception change because of altered thinking? What comes first, our senses focusing outward or our internal mental processes? What is primarily determining, living through our senses or being inside our heads? We know what technology is making of us and we have largely become a head tripping species, unfortunately for many people, existence is little more than being talking heads in our cyborgian interactions with both friends and outliers.

Einstein told us that everything had changed with the coming of nuclear weapons, except how we think about the concrete realities of the world, the human condition and life itself at risk. Einstein's admonition has been ignored and humanity provided assurance through the politics of "Mutually Assured Destruction" and our being publicly redirected and redefined via consumerism in relentless overdrive. Planetary convulsions throughout the spectrum of what is now commonly referred to as climate crisis are more occurrent, visceral and immediate than the fantastical horror of nuclear holocaust. From this, it appears, there is a wider opening and openness to change how we think and in potentially asking who we are and even why.

At this moment in terrestrial history, one thing is certain. There is an imperative, an Earth imperative, that we change. As Earth's dominate species, trained in ubiquitous disregard and unfeeling abusiveness, the human footprint and consequences of cumulative rampage are everywhere. The implications involve us all and the solutions to this complex problematic require us all. Canadian environmentalist David Suzuki spoke a truth that gets to the heart of this troubling matter by saying, "The climate crisis is a human crisis."

So, what are we going to do about this, about us, or what are not going to do by continuing denial, by holding back or refusing to face up to and get to doing what needs to be done? Procrastination is only an evasive form of refusal, perhaps attached to a concealed wish for the challenge to disappear of its own volition if only it is put off long enough and ignored?

But life is dynamic, the Earth, as a living entity, is dynamic. To move from inaction to correct action may be to emerge as avatars of relationships, conscientious keepers and ecosophic guardians.

Across generations we have risen, unthinkingly come and gone, as a breed apart. This is something we are not, but which has disastrously been accepted and pursued out of false ideas, unexamined assumptions, expectations, reasoning, unreasoning, and wrong perceptions. Both human ignorance and arrogance have led to where we are. Human immaturity has allowed us to believe in entitlement, to believe that what is false is true, that what is convenient is alright at whatever cost, and that everything will work out because, after all, this place, and our placement here, is transient. We are inheritors of ideas of salvation promising a New Heaven and a New Earth, the "other place" to which the faithful are to be transported after the final laying waste of what is given. In this context it has regularly been held as heretical to pursue the ideals of Heaven as potentials of this very Earth, as goals on the continuum of the here and now. This despite all evidence informing us that Earth is the only home any of us has real experience of.

Because of such ideas, and this importantly is but one of the keys to Western thinking, we are in the burgeoning predicament of our distressed human condition and the traumatized realities of this one only Earth.

So, we are not a breed apart. We are rather participants in the diverse inclusiveness of planetary life. We do not live on the Earth but abide within the Earth and the comprehensive spectrum of elemental structures, biotic systems and diversity which has evolved into a vital, vibrant, and intricate unity of diversity, which by us is continuously being assailed, disrupted, reduced, imperiled. The rending of life structures, atmospheric and biotic systems, regulating oceans, driving planetary wind and moisture cycles, the chemical composition of the air life depends on, remain largely out of focus outside of scientific communities. But the Big Picture, along with local weather and the rest that is immediate are two perspectives of the whole reality and both require accurate and honest response.

Yes, we are responsible to Earth and to Humanity, to future generations human and transhuman alike, to self and to other, and integrally to the outward reach of otherness. Our responsibility is to cultivate, with sensitive urgency, a culture of response-abilities flourishing throughout a civilization of relationships. If not this, if continuing in the encasement of isolation and overconsumption, depletion, collapse is already waiting to overwhelm us and cut off our children.

Earth is in need and we, as inhabitants of Earth with no home alternative actual or fantastical, are in need. To satisfy any need requires honest acknowledgement, recognition, and clarity – requires a direction leading to appropriate action. A key alternative to cataclysmic anticipation is in changing how we think: developing alternatives in what, why, how and who. The ability to do such is a signature of our collective intelligence, the blessed curse and cured blessing evolution has bestowed upon us.

As thinking changes, our priorities will also change, moving further from what we erroneously believe we deserve and far too often out of dumbness, numbness, and moral bankruptcy demand, to more belongingly relearning what we love, what by love we are capable of and of making a mortal of love to thrive and pass from generation to generation. Therein can life transpire through acts of beauty – the prolific doing of what is right for life because it is right to do so.

Entrenched and reactionary power structures, impositions set against nature, coupled with obsolete concepts and erroneous and endangering attitudes of entitlement resist the changes that are needed. These obstacles are real and yet to be overcome.

But now, as if by way of a majority report, I think it is correct, or in process of becoming correct, to state this: The majority of those alive now already recognize that change is required to move into what is best and most possible to keep Earth as a habitable homestead, a living planet, and to work together to assure that dignity is conditional for the future of global life.

Love The Earth – Gaia-Earth

...depth is the primordial dimension because we are entirely in depth...
we are within the biosphere... Laura Sewall *

Burrow down, dig deep. What waits there deep within, in the buried core of dreamtime-memory and sacred vision, the outer world now has pressing need of – needing you and me and all other pivot-points, being points of light.

Learn to be still, receptive, and quiet, radiant, and composed. Grow comfortable with sharing silence: not empty silence that breeds lethargy and conspires with indifference, but rather the bountiful, living energy of plenum-silence – cosmic while yet intimately blended into the everyday forms and forces of earthly creation.

Do not be afraid of either who or what you are. Throughout torments and tempests of time, over many generations, we have been lied to. Now, out of custom, we are generationally guilty of repeating pernicious and dimension-diminishing lies.

Change your habits and you change the content of your heritage. Change the parameters and content of heritage and you change perceptions and contours of the future. Past and future are collected here like seeds of yesterday and tomorrow on the alive palm of the present moment.

Change your habits from false to authentic, from the bogus privileges of decadent alienation and self-indulgent but self-betraying isolation, to become naturally reconnected and passionately involved. Change your direction and put aside conflicting differences and learned suspensions and suppressions of recognition.

In the past, only on the battlefields of war was there total commensality. The war dead and those awaiting the largescale onslaught of murder succumb to war death in common. In the near future, the waging of peace, and a restoration of stability and sanity to this ravaged planet, will require, with unprecedented urgency and tenacity, a surpassing embrace of natural wisdom and compassionate commensality. Commensality as an eating and feeding love feast of responsible inclusiveness.

At a time coming toward us steadily, all who are alive will live on the frontlines: denying or defending life, extinguishing, or participating in the sacredness of life. Let red and black, the brown, yellow and white in solidarity compose a banner to hoist up, to celebrate beneath together. Let there be the handprint of a human child in center of this flag of Gaia colors, to show to ourselves and those who follow after "we are trusting and relational and, in our betterment, this seeding for enlightenment is truly who we are."

Love Gaia-Earth. Without the passion of our pathos, without our engaged and enduring connectivity, the actuals of Earth, breathing with and within and through us, could shortly perish, can someday be no more.

Now, if so moved, say with me these signature words of renaissance:

"I for one, despite realities of evil, believe with an unburdened heart in the human adventure and the evolutionary integrity of this life-place, our Earth home. While I do not submit to maintenance at all costs of a profane, vulgarizing and ceaselessly devouring, civilization, I do believe in the empowering emergence of mature and responsible species possibilities – of a future revolution out of inner evolution of human beings who carry in the grounding dimensions of personhood the legacy of the human animal as well as the virtual-into-actual ecosophy of human angel."

Know these truths then: There are three requirements to undertake the healing journey to mend, in each one's part and power, the broken circle of creation.

Easy to speak but arduous, demanding of diligence, dedication: you must reconcile, as polarities of integrity, the oppositions inside of you, wedding what opposes to what is opposed; you must fall in love outwardly; you must, through your love – your Earth angel fire – live the passion of pathos, the everywhere of infinite sensitivities that unify in dynamic interplay the living weave, of forms and forces, of cosmos and Gaia; of the visible and invisible; of the now known and the yet to become known.

The shaman in the blood and ancient interface of soul with life's grounding dimension knows how to shapeshift through acts of beauty beyond mere rigors of adaptation. Therein the world of science and the mystic meet. Learn again to trust. Here once say with me please: "We love the Earth. Ours is a strong, pure, and sustaining love. A love that cannot, and will not, be bought or sold."

I started out here with a simple admonition: Love the Earth – Gaia-Earth. Now a Long Note of Continuing Relevance: The name Gaia, Mother of All Life, comes down to us from the archaic period of ancient Greece. It is a Goddess name, a name that has been reintroduced into popular speech by environmental scientist James Lovelock. Lovelock is the author of Gaia Theory and it is worthwhile taking a minute or so to review what that theory entails. I do not know if James Lovelock imputes goddess status to Gaia or proves sentience, although neither need be excluded from serious discussion and I am personally inclined toward affirmation. My ecosophy is largely immersed in personating, "making person" as was defined in Shakespeare's time, and believe that species to species and interdimensional communication is possible in so far as we retrieve the lost language that unites all entities and forces of creation. But what Gaia Theory does assert is this: Planet Earth is a living organism, a gestalt of life within which the sum of the parts exceeds the parts themselves, forming a distinct unit of dynamic identity.

There are two notable characteristics of every living organism and we may take these characteristics as actual signatures of identity. First, what is alive naturally and spontaneously functions to maintain and extend its life. Second, that a living organism reacts protectively to danger and assault and the more developed the organism, the greater the response and more intense the protective fury to defend continuance. Easy to invoke images of a trapped and wounded tiger turning on its tormentors or of a mother bear raging against intruders invading her territory, threatening her cubs.

We humans are the tormentors and we the intruders and it would be best for us and a habitable future if we desist from these roles, learn to let go and let be, reenter relationships of honoring, practice humility and ritualize reverence. Reverence for the sacred circle of evolutionary diversity, for the interweave of biotic communities. Reverence for All Mothering Gaia, a living matrix wherein beauty and abundance flourish and democratize through Her self-regulating systems into the inclusive provisioning for species generations and balancing cycles recurrence.

I am not a scientist or in agreement with certain conclusions of James Lovelock. My personal passion is more adapted to the ancient Homeric Hymn from which Gaia's name and status first reach us over centuries, and too the poetic explorations of Robert Bly in *News of the Universe – Poems of Twofold Consciousness*. In that Sierra Club Book, Bly poses the following question:

"This book asks one question over and over: How much consciousness is the poet willing to grant to trees or hills or creatures not a part of his own species?"

As an eco-poet and shamanic storyteller, I identify with this question and have had time to experience the implications of holding creative discourse with the variegated otherness of the natural world – natural otherness traditionally memorialized in pre-literate ecological cultures and as memories embedded in us through archetypes and ancestral narratives. For me, the question is a Gaia question and there are multiple choices of imaginative responses and appropriate behavioral answers. For me, whether the time is of tender beauty or tempest fury, this and every Gaia question is a probing of love. If to ask of Gaia is love-asking, it is equally a sacred inquiry.

Here I am, come full circle, back to where I was before. Be more open. Become more porous. Embrace more, being more vulnerable and sensitively inclusive. Crying for a vision is a wisdom approach to prayer. Love the Earth – Gaia Earth: Love Her.

*The Skill of Ecological Perception by Laura Sewall from ECOPSYCHOLOGY: Restoring the Earth Healing the Mind.

Meditations

Leafy Bower

If you go out to the leafy bower to pray and the God or Goddess you pray to is but One, Lady-Lord Creator and Wild, because the natural constitution of Earth was ever intended to be teeming wilderness, a bubbling cauldron, a percolating laboratory of evolutionary life...

If you go out under the leafy bower to lift your souls in joy to Great Spirit, to Cosmic Creator, to the Dream Maker of space, dimensions, mysteries and time, those who are opposed to greening will call you Pagan – even if merely meaning Paganized Catholic or Paganized Protestant, Pagan-Moslem or Pagan-Jew – and say you are worshipping Pan, shaggy Pan of the wild thighs, or Angus Og, or Mother Gaia, or even the eternal enemy itself, goat footed Satan, with tail retained from the animal realm.

But when they say it, using words of contempt and condemnation, laugh with the saying and invite the angry, threatened, to step out with you along the Beauty Way, with trees above and sky above trees and the dark painted skin of fertile Earth greeting underneath naked feet, and the stones inside of Living Earth (as if bones of skeleton holding your flesh in place) and roots living down below...

Let them hear you sing and show them how you hold no mistaught desire to remain a breed apart, but through singing nature, praise, and the living world you aspire to become again a part of all being – noble, alive, and free.

Show to the cruelty of past men and the greed of men present; those who have spit on the Earth and into their children's faces and onto the glory of Gaia; that when they call you Pagan – even if merely meaning Paganized Catholic or Paganized Protestant, Pagan-Moslem or Pagan-Jew – each of them you will teach to dance with the Green Flame of Life, which is none other than God or Goddess as Goddess-God dreaming among us, and the Green Flame of Life being Council Fire in the House of Spirit, set out without a single wall to block out light or darkness, wind or rain, winged or four legged, great or small.

Let the others, too, see your faces and your hands, feet, and your drums and the green bower light that filters down and the pure gift of light shining from within you. Say to them there that you do not require a name to your calling, for you are invested in love, in bowers and seas, of flowers and beetles and butterflies and bees, and have discovered, gratefully and with great humility, that this Living Earth is home. And this home, a fertility of great prayer, is Holy Ground.

First Democracy

I am here. This is me. My hands at the ends of my arms twirl, making circular motions. My soul is lively, my spirit thrives in motion. My feet at the ends of my legs form patterns, pictographs of where I have been, my direction, where I am heading. My footsteps follow me, and I am remembered.

Earth – I am walking.

The way goes out like this before. The way goes out like this behind. I am part of what is out before. I am part of what is behind. I am part of it all and all of it is part of me. Earth and the life of Earth surrounds me. Conjoining as far as the eye can see, to be conjoined as far as my legs will take me. Truth is in good Ecosophy. There is truth in these words. There is Gospel, meaning Good News, in the urgency of what is said here.

Crookedly the paths meander, passages curving through space and time. Pleasure is to be found along the journey. Wonderment springs up at intervals, nests, and ceremonies of the wayside. Occasions of lamentation.

Deep in the repository of my soul are stored fins to swim in rivers to the oceans. Deep in the repository of my soul wings await to fly on winds. Quiet. Listen. The sounds of fluttering, all but lost amid the persistence of breath and heartbeat, and mechanical thunder. All but lost in the clamor that time has become.

My hands make circular motions. Watch now. I fly atop trees, between the metamorphic circus of atmospheric clouds. My heart, which can betray or affirm us, fills with songs of freedom. The whale knows more songs than I do. Bless the whale for

45

singing, the flights of birds and cosmic dreamers.

My hands make circular motions. I help to shape whatever greets me; what greets me gives shape to who I am. Shadow too records memories of life's communions, broken treaties weighted off against enchantments of connections.

I am here. This is me. Out along the Red Path, learning from experience, gleaming from the harvest of first democracy – from first day, hour, minute, breath, when eyes opened, mouth opened, tongue licked delicate lips, fists tightened, unclenched to clutch at light and air – experiencing what it is to become a human being, Earthling, a person, a presence, on the Living Earth.

Whatever I touch touches me before I get there. Turning toward is communication. This is how it is here. How truth is lived on this Living Earth.

Do not let truth vanish. Do not let Earth die.

Tao and Dharma

The world is falling apart. Again, the world falls apart. Admit it. All the time, all around, something of the weather, a chaos, a curse, of human violence. And wherever disaster strikes next there is pain, anguish, loss, and suffering.

Give thanks for being alive. Whenever you feel peace of mind, of heart and soul, send the message of blessings outward. Even in the trembling give thanks for being here. Say, this is here and now. Do not be one of the deniers, misguided in deception, in delusion. Do not be an escapist. It is unbecoming. Dignity does not adhere to what is unbecoming. Do not drop into the abyss.

Ask forgiveness. Seek to be forgiven for ignorance and the cruelty of humankind. Once, long lost in common past, we were integral, a part of creation. Long since, we are not good for this Earth and the diversity of Earth's structures and creatures.

The world is falling apart. Again, the world falls apart. Admit it. We are the dis-eased excess weighing oppressively on the bosom of the Earth.

Ask forgiveness of a newly shed pinecone, of an enduring stone. Stand on a shore, seashore, or river's bank, showing your sorrow, saying you are sorry. Chant or sing or shed some of your profound tears of broken love. If you are not a willing part of human madness, let nature know how ardently you long for return.

As the world falls apart do not fall apart with it. Rather, where there is darkness, radiate a light of compassion. Where there is violence, be a practitioner of nonviolence. Breathing beatitude, be a practitioner of peace. Then, where there is rage, and lashing out, injury and confusion, be the choice of trust.

The world falls apart. Evidence is obvious. How do we stop this? How do we reverse the terrible and terrifying process? We will not save the self-destroying world. You cannot; I cannot. And yet, if each of us who are warriors of gentle spirit and lovers in affirming passion measure the configuration of immediacy and strive to rescue even our small piece of the living fabric, we will be doing all that is in our power to do.

Who can say what is heard in the pathos of honesty? Who can say what is felt in the vibrations of choices? Make sure mind is clear and heart pure. There is strength in clarity. There is strength in purity. Living beside one another in the Way and the Law, unity emerges. Organically, with patience, unity consciously unites, celebrates in spontaneities, celebrates the enlightenment of evolution.

Fitting into what is falling apart is surrender to the illusions of separation, to the status of existing as fragment. Follow rather the Tao of reverence. Invite to communion; seek completion. Abide in the Dharma of creation. Nature establishes diversity, moderation, patience, placement, and systemic interdependence. No "I" without "Thou." No consciousness without context. Awaken out of ego, emerge into eco.

If you believe you are listened to, continue in this dialogue of mutuality and hallowing. Listening happens – remain alert. Both action and intention matter when you turn weakness into humility and courage into dedication.

What does it matter what name you attribute to your Listener? That name bears your signature. Planted in the root cellar of identity, there grows the hidden treasure of your soul. You are a child of this planet. Be at home here. Be lover – ever soulful, deeply rooted.

If a stranger estranged from truth questions: "What are you doing with your life?" Meet the challenge in the moment. Respond: "I sing the world – both affliction and renewal, the broken and mending, both barren plot and sowing."

If a stranger estranged from truth laughs at your reply, say quietly, "I too practice the yoga of laughter! I am a dancer of Tao. I am a poet of Dharma. My vulnerability is my garment of light. Every day I do a little sewing."

This then is my mandala. This then is who I am. The world is falling apart. My soul is a lotus; I am not a shard. Not broken glass. I am not falling. And you?'

Poet's Love and Samurai Sword

Who walks with me? Let them put on their walking shoes. Walk lightly but with dedicated urgency and joy.

It is not the "meager-I" of me that calls you by your name, but the voice of the Earth addressing each and many who are attentive to the dynamic imperative of Earth-mutuality. What we have referred to as Heaven and believed to be betterment beyond is now a plaintive, passionate resonance of memory in the evolutionary energies of living things.

What is your image of the Holy? What do you feel when feeling is empowered to expression in the presence of Earth's diversity – Her forms and Her children?

Who talks with me? Who holds in one heart, on one tongue, the spark of poetic love and tenderness and the samurai's sword? Let words be honest, measured and ennobling between us. Let your tongue be rooted in the connective awakening of your soul.

Earth as she has grown in supportive complexity is radical with amazement. What radically amazes excites to articulation, invites into dialogue. Who dares to let the magic of Earth work midwifery upon human vulnerability?

Do not assume more than what and where you are; do not be less in conveyance than this context which enfolds you.

Be humble as you are courageous, in making heard, changing perception, and bringing into focus this agony, the hope, the quivering and pulsating, this longing of the lost and endangered, the unheard, the unconsidered motion, motive, and the unseen.

Who stands in the circle of reverence for life before, next, and round about me? Let us join hands.

The body too, flesh of the ground; bone of Earth-stones; is metamorphic to become prayer. Let us be joyous in our repentance. Let us be prosperous with appreciation.

There is no more genuine profit than in Acts of Beauty: doing what is right because it is right. There is no more authentic and authenticating wealth, or health, or sense of worth, identity, or belonging, than joining the caravan of the mystic in collective return to the Beauty Way.

Eco-Dharma

Follow the repetitions of patterns. Do not permit yourself the escapism of boredom. Boredom is a modern dysfunction. It is part of the urban disease of removal from the rhythms and cycles of nature. Boredom grows as a fungus out of the debris of anxiety.

An awakened person who frequents nature outside of civilization; whoever let's go and let's be and is immersed; knows no experience of boredom. But is at-one with the relaxed and balanced Tao of flow. It is shameful waste for those who are trapped in deception and conflicted daily in existential torment between anxiety and boredom.

Follow the repetitions of patterns while you come simultaneously to utter amazement – to life as wonderment abounding and as first democracy – in the uniqueness of entities: snowflakes, persons, raindrops, and roses. Nature delivers simultaneously in uniqueness and patterns.

Ancient sages of cultures without clutter looked at creation this way. It was from them, the Shining Ones of Shinto and Tao, that Buddha mastered the art of perception. How soul sees the world and how the transhuman context of the human feels within the integrity of all that is other, this is the mastery of perception.

Honesty of perception requires the double vision of union out of polarity, and also requires patience. Out of the patient balancing of polarities integrity actualizes freedom and inner harmony flowers into compassion.

If Buddha had lacked the courage of true seeing, how could

Buddha have become Buddha and earned the endearment of compassionate? And Gandhi, had he not had similar courage and the integral simultaneity of patterns and uniqueness how would Gandhi have deserved the title bestowed upon him by his people – Mahatma, Great Soul?

Follow the repetitions of patterns and you will learn justice. Affirm reverence for uniqueness and you democratize dignity. In the Beauty Way and through acts of beauty, adhere to unity through diversity and you abide in peace.

Gestalt of Love's Completion
on the Day of the Solar Eclipse 21 August 2017

If a man can speak, in honesty and integrity, with another man If a woman can speak, in honesty and integrity, with another woman If a woman can speak with a man If a man can speak with a woman;

If a human being can speak with creatures of the Earth (this Gaia-Earth) with those of land, those of air, those of waters – rivers, streams, lakes and seas;

If a human being can speak with spirit worlds (worlds within worlds within worlds – spheres – seed-spheres, dream-spheres, womb-spheres), the elemental spirits, native to wisdom and the wild, the angels, magnificent and minor, of guidance, grace and glory, and the planets and combusting stars;

If a human being, a person, can speak, personally, in honesty and integrity, with reverence for life and in deep humility, with the Lord and Lady of Creation, the Wild God of Heaven on Earth, storm and spring, the Green Goddess of pollen and flora, fauna and autumn;

If all of this is so, has become or is becoming, that person of many blessings is in the power zone, recovering dialects of the lost language – keeping the vision in motion – the Great Vision of Life in Balance to full-on Cosmic Harmony.

Here, on the day of solar eclipse, 2017, I have spoken quietly on the Gestalt of Love's Completion. I have spoken of democracy democratizing deliverance. I have spoken of truth-force maturing into liberation. Those who have ears hear the resonance. Those with eyes assist vision. Those with souls live in feeling. All such abide poetically within this Living Earth. Ah... Here comes the sun!

Walking Back Zarathustra

When Zarathustra was thirty years old he left his home and the lake of his home and went into the mountains. Here he enjoyed his spirit and his solitude, and for ten years did not tire of it.
But at last a change came over his heart... --Nietzsche

When Zarathustra came down from the mountains, he met the people living below and spoke with them. The prophet said, "From a single spark the world becomes conflagration."

The people who heard were shocked by the pronouncement of this peculiar stranger. Some among them replied, "Is the world to become dust and ashes? Who are you?" questioned others. "Would you walk among us and bring destruction? What is this terrible spark you dare speak to us of?" The prophet observed the terror on the faces of the people and laughed. "What a waste and pity," he told himself, "so accustomed are they to being downcast and living in fear."

Zarathustra looked around, for a crowd was now gathered, and he spoke boldly. He said, "What is already dust and ashes will fulfil itself with or without miracle. While those who are seeds will blossom, as mercy, into colorful perfumes. Those who are trees will bear fruit. Flowers will inspire hearts; fruit will nourish souls."

Most standing before the prophet were puzzled and speechless. But one spoke up, beyond confusion, tauntingly saying, "All of this from a single spark! What then is this spark that can turn the world of combating light and shadow into fire?"

"Friend," the prophet answered, "I recognize your courage.

Then let me tell you. In the beginning when Creator Goddess-God set the incandescence of being in motion, unleashing power out of withdrawal, from the inscrutable depths of the mystery of androgynous nothingness, this spark that I have foretold is the same as the spark that moved all that ever was, or is, and will ever be."

Most now struggled with this riddle, hunched, or shrugged and turned away. Some were convinced the prophet was mad; delusional from having lived too long in solitude among the mountains. They wondered smugly: Has Zarathustra not heard that God is dead? Or that we mortals have replaced the Ancient of Days with the Will to Power? We have submitted to hording and ignorance, are without compass, dimensionless, yet we are content. We will not question. We seek no communal fire to set our comfort and convenience ablaze."

A few remained awestruck, however, touched by some reality deeper than isolation, convention, forgetfulness. These latter were those who sensed the presence of lost language in the prophet's words. They were to become Zarathustra's companions, as the spark foretold was re-birthing in the fertile depths of their souls.

Some of the companions believed the spark was love and the prophet had come down to the people to return the world to love. For the world, they knew, was already far gone into hardness and hatred and into violence. Steadily, under the cult and culture of desolation, the rootless world was reduced to wasteland.

Others of the companions believed the spark was freedom and the prophet had come down to the people to set the world free from fear and darkness, and from the abyss of history, the past, and the fatality of human self-reference. These knew that only the greatest desire; the fire that leaps into belly and head from the furnace of the Creator; could reverse the world's enslavement to affliction and conflict; to surrendering to the degrees of death, and to the dictates of death, devoid of beatitudes: existence without reverence, resistance, without rebellion and hallowing.

But which group is right here: those who stolidly turned away? Those whose faces fell as they showed the prophet their backs? Or which of the two camps of companions, and what common ground would unite them? Is love the key to liberation, or liberation the striving way, the rite of passage, to set love free?

Configurations of a Change Mandala

You: Yes, I come talking with you. You feel the Earth, the living Earth, this Gaia of integral, interweaving, biotic communities. You know in your distress how destruction is happening. Toward what end imbalance accelerations.

You face the human problem, the false identity, the calamitous folly. You know the danger is real; the threat, incessant, continuously increases. You do not hide from it.

Your gnosis derives from your sensitive consciousness. Sensitivity of consciousness, distinguishable from what is merely informational, prioritizes out of empathetic response-ability (feeling the sight and thought of affliction and alternatives): your core-immediacy envisioning response.

This is significant. The dimensions of significance – the ways in which openness and affinities are allowed – should not be ignored; no more than empathy should be boxed off from intuition. To ignore dimension is to reduce the vitality and the inter-dimensional continuum of life. That is a technique of authoritarian politics. To box off, or cut empathy away, is to render relationships pointless and fellow creature feelings aberrant. When there is no love there are no relationships and where relationships are denied and broken, how indifferently easy to exterminate, to force extinction!

For all of this, your sensitive consciousness is but a skin level intimation of an individuating visionary gestation; a unique difference pulsating, shaping through nature into natural power. The intention being to introduce newness, an agent of instinct and spirit, maturity, into our species sequence.

Now listen I am sending these words to you, who toss in sleepless nights, who gaze into dark mirrors and wander lonely streets. Existential and conflicted: believing yourself a shard in an urban labyrinth of fragmented glass.

Because of what gestates within, you seem, even in your clouded eyes, to be an anomaly. But is the anomaly an outsider, a social pariah, or a promise? Some wisdom of the unknown lifting to become known! Some substance of the invisible materializing to become visible!

In the interior difference of you (let us point to your intolerance of the common levels of violence, hatred, obscenity, dishonesty of thought and action; indifference and ignorance): are you a figure, configuring in a still formulating Change Mandala? Secreted, perhaps even to yourself, are you part of future-present preparations of an Earth based metamorphic redemption?

Is Earth and Spirit's subtle response to the human wars of extinctions the Rainbow Warrior of biotic democracy actualizing through you? The Green Troubadour of sanity episodically birthing out of your burgeoning Ecosophy?

Questions of this sort are significant. You should ask these questions seriously, deep down in your passion and humility (your potential to "cry for vision," as Natives would say), and make of your Earth invested vision a way of life. Now is not a time to be immature or abrupt. Now is not a time to be hysterical or afraid.

Bravely ask: Does the "hidden treasure" of your identity constitute an evolutionary presence? Are you a love-radical inviting life back to life in balance? Inviting our dis-integral species back to sanity?

If you are dismayed and puzzled as to why you are, existing as we do in the here and now of a traumatic world, you should ask the questions ardently, and not leave your life to marginalized obscurity and happenstance. Despite the dishonesty of techno-time, awakened identity may yet be destiny. Only ask not for an assurance of answers. Remain in asking; refrain from seeking shelter in escapist fictions and narcissistic fantasy.

Do not allow yourself to become answer heavy. Do not blow your mind along the way, thinking on how special you are. Do not become that fixation of the pendulum! That fixation that precludes fossilization.

Rather, consider the process of seed becoming flower or tree. Practice the subtle discipline of growth. The way of evolution is serious. You will be summoned when you are ripe. In the meantime, heed the water, the land, the air. Observe the sky-movement of birds and the twin directional aspiration of trees.

Learn to fall in love outward, in the encircling directions of afflicted nature. Live for life beyond your own. Only in Big Love, in Abiding Desire, in the Big Responsibility of Belonging, is there enduring purpose, peace of mind, solace for your soul.

What I am telling you about here pertains to spontaneity of soul – of your soul rising to bear in part the needed change in perception, thinking, feeling, valuing, and belonging. Belonging has been lost by our aggression and our isolation. The evolution that would return us, that desires and moves inside you, is a human revolution. It is not about superiority contra inferiority but may well have to do with a simultaneity of pioneering and return. Say: This is Buddha beneath the tree of enlightenment. This is Saint Paul on the road to Damascus; Saint Teresa of Avila enraptured. It is entirely adoration of this Earth – Mother Gaia in process of being returned to the queenship of beauty, abundance, and stability – to life.

The nature of each entity functions as a law. This law can be broken and often is, ruining the entity, causing calamity. In calamity is suffering. The entity-law can be fulfilled and that, like hallelujah, signals harmony. Innate to harmony is abundance and joy.

On this Living Earth, it is evolution that unfolds; confirms or dismisses the laws of Being. This is ancient process. It is medicine in the old way of magic, magic in the way of medicine. Yet the outcome, out of you, expects to come forth as hope, vitality, renew!

I call this the sea working on a seashell; a star being initiated into starlight by the star-spangled cosmos. I call this the configuring Configurations of a Change Mandala; both mystery and dance: offering of a new paradigm rooted in a mega, that is, superordinate, spirit garden of infinite figures.

You may, in your awakening, name it whatever you please. Only be sure in doing so you speak only truth. Truth in the voice of trust.

Voice of Andrea Bocelli

I am as sweet as the voice of Andrea Bocelli I am as deep as the bottomless miracle of Shakespeare as solid with sublime marvel as stones of Michelangelo as full as the Tao of Beethoven with power to wed the symphonic stars of heaven with choral oceans, moon-tides forests and elder-sage trees of this living Earth

I am as small as the mustard seed of Jesus, a parable containing the complexity of Bach, a prayer as humble as the birds of Saint Francis (you know the way that Giotto shows us Francisco's simplicity) As holy as the dancing laughter of wise and wandering Baal Shem Tov, I am as righteous with visions as prophets Isaiah the promise-maker as Black Elk and Einstein and immortal Elijah, as big with mandala-dreaming as Willie Blake, and Corbin, and Doctor Jung

I am a trinity of animal, angel human wise but foolish, foolish with wisdom both clowning and striving to become human and holy

I am as sweet, as sweet as the voice of Andrea Bocelli: beauty of a man become song.

"I am" empathetic, shape-shifting poems are an old tradition, once especially prominent among the cultures of Native Americans and Celts, of both Ireland and Britain, which is to say, among people whose lives were connected to nature and seasons and cosmic cycles. Those who composed and recited to remember what Spirit reveals, and who built to ritualize connection and participation between Earth Humanity and Heaven.

So now, friend, make an "I am" poem of your own; celebrate

through its creative throbbing and select accomplishments of our shared humanity! Think ancient. Feel mandala. Origami in time and space, folding and unfolding beyond human comprehension. Not beyond fascination: Imagine. Be different with your words from my words. Be utterly more completely you!

How wonderful to step and skip, hop, run, swim and fly beyond the burden and nihilistic terror of human comprehension!

I am the eternal life-force, truth-force: desire... I am the eternal, sheer, naked, vulnerable, living soul. I am The Tree in the garden of your dreams. I am that wind blowing off clouds playing out light and dark over your footsteps, along your pathways.

I am your music, your heartbeat, your song that sings – and I am happy to make you happy. the heart that beats, song that sings, happy, happy to make you happy. You – being who you are! Resonate. Recall...

I am part of all this, of all. I am of that...all. I am, bodied and souled, an angel of love. That. This. The he. The she.

A prism. An entity. What is spoken partnering with what cannot be spoken. What is seen and what desires to remain unseen. Deep, deep in the reaches. Fathoms of recess. The Forgotten; Rediscovered. The Silence. The Whispering out of Silence.

I am that eternal, of this living soul. I am Tree in the garden of your dreams. I am wind blowing off clouds that darken, scintillating, darkening, and lighting, your solitude: meandering in The Way; way that is yours. My way. Your way. I am music, you, your music, ours, your heartbeat, ours; song that you sing, happy song... happy to make you happy. I am of all this. Why not that? One grain of sand, one drop of honey, and multiplicity of our angels of Earth Eros. The Beauty of a man become song, friend... Friend! Friend: s-h-h-h-h!

I am as the voice of Andrea Bocelli.

Circle Maker

Once we humans were wise. We are no longer wise. Once we humans were few and there was, once upon a time, a sort of democracy of Earth wisdom. Now we are many, far, far too many, and endangering to the life realms of this beautifully evolved planet. A life-sphere, that is what Earth became before us. That is the truth we now threaten.

Once in the way-back we humans understood, as native and natural intuition, that to join in circle is to participate in the revelation of sacred space. A circle too encompasses an interval of time, making of the joining in circle an entering into sacred time. In circle, space and time are shaped circular. God or Goddess, attendant spirits and creatures of ordinary magic are dreamed of, adored, spoken of and offered adoration in round.

A circle is facing inward and readily a celebration. A solemn or a lively ritual, sending out, symbolizing the thanksgiving of remembering the delicate and yet hardy spiral of questing and the endless knot of pilgrimage. That is a truth wanting our touch, our toughness, tenderness, and our love.

Standing in circle is way of perception – the way the human soul looks at life and creation, feeling through seeing the living realities of land, sky, and sea.

Looking into the curved gathering of friends; circle as a ring of bonding; is a realizing of shared intention and committing each self to this act of beauty in the presence of other looking and breathing human bodies – the diversity of colors, shapes, lights, shadows, rhythms and impressions – and the traits, talents, dreams and imaginations of receptive, wakeful, life-conscious faces.

In circle one can receive the images of other human beings, the visions across rocks and grasses, among winds passing and abiding trees: all this without fear or distrust, without anxiety or disgust. Death is linear as is pointlessness. But the circle points in every direction and gently transfigures death.

Right here, here and right now, speaking of Earth wisdom and blessings of circles, uplifted I recall from the Celts, Macha, sweet-water Brigit and Deirdre of the Sorrows. I recall from Native American tribes Chief Seattle, Wovoka, dreamer of Ghost Dance, Black Elk and Standing Bear, of Lakota. To name is to honor.

Here, right here and right now, searching to return in commune to the wisdom and the blessings of circle, with a fire bright in my heart and head, I call across the ley lines of the sacred to you, and would bestow on you the healing name of Circle Maker. You, friend, upon whom the sacred duty unites with desire, like a butterfly, wing-footed, alighting, by the grace of nature, on petals of a rose.

Free of Clutter

Before there was a world of far too many things – the floating world and world of lost treasures – there was the culture of breathing, breath was full, sustaining, pure; there was the culture of word, words were simple, dimensional, direct, clear; the culture of vision, and visions were of light and dark and comingling of light and dark, and there were living shapes and myriad colors. Living ones of soul and spirit breathed into the world narratives of creation, telling generations that out of this came that and from one the other, and in the All – behold! – each to each conjoins.

Now in the broken world – world of psyche fragments and razor-sharp emotional shards – there is noise and rubbish; nostrils suck in fumes, tongues are coated with filth, blood-ooze, mind's uncleanness, and people with aggressive and irresponsible pride practice forgetfulness and the entertainments of addictive violence.

If today's individuals have choice between owning the newest model, most luxuriant car or practicing austerities, sitting beneath a tree of enlightenment, maybe one of a million would choose in a moment, as a pearl of eternity, the serene meditation of light and life, over the speed and metallic painted power of the degrees of death.

If this is so, is it really a surprise that heaven is confused, fevered and weary of the modern, and the Earth in disgust of a dreadful labor gives birth to rage?

The ignorant along with the so-called learned talk carelessly of karma. Someone near, perhaps a neighbor, says, "We are all going to hell in a hand-basket." Tragically, for wild and the children, even legions of the damned no longer recall what a handbasket is, or how to leap from one and land in one piece on the ground. And when another here cries out in panic that "The barbarians are coming!" – why, take note of this irony – barbarians among us sheepishly look around, grinning, as they kick the dust over their shadows.

To whom, in our chaos, does it matter if said: From the hair of the fertile woman grew herbs and plants, flowers and trees; from fingers of the imaging man issued energy spheres of God's-eye stars? Of course, such is of the Thousand and One Androgynous Nights, when primordial two were primordial one, called tales of Purusha, called tales of Adam Kadmon; when there were, in the dreaming, free of clutter, free of thingness, breath, word, vision – sustaining, simple, profound, pure.

A Wild God

God turned my way. God spoke before me. God said: "I am tired of these houses of worship, the walled buildings of men. They are beautiful. Some are exquisite, some even sublime. And they have served a purpose.

"But I who am beyond walls am weary of these dividing walls. What is a mind set against itself? Or what a mouth devouring the limbs of its body?

"I long to be out in the wind. And I am the wind.

"I long to be under stars and the deep space cradling stars. And I am stars, the cradle, the cradling, and the dark mystery of surrounding and gestating space and time.

"I long to be in sunlight and moon-glow. And I am the light and the glow – the radiant.

"I long to be out in rain. I who send rain and am falling rain and the weeping of angels.

"I long to be in snow. And I am the scripture of snow and the calligraphy both of frost and water. Seasons of holding and the seasons of letting go.

"I long to journey freely in warmth, wafting over many lands. And I am the fire and the breath moving the myriads of creation. The elements and the many walks."

I heard these words. I felt them as feeling words: the words of a wild God with Goddess form. Longing for a change in relationships.

I and Thou

I open my mind; we share our thoughts. I open my mouth; we share our words. I open my heart; we share our human feelings of life. I open soul: here I am in the dynamic of becoming. Before me is who you are, metamorphic in the mystic flow. Mystery between us in the unconscious; outwardly unfolding, we envision together. I and Thou.

The dream of freedom is as old as human time. Freedom from want and fear. Freedom from hurt and woe. Freedom to become the "who" of being we each and every one are endowed with power to become. Freedom from and freedom for. Not to be denigrated or to denigrate. Not to be violated and not to violate. Freedom as a form of social contract; freedom as a norm.

The dream of peace is as old as human sorrow. We are Earth-walkers from horizon to horizon: from primal caverns to skyward summits. We who are dreamers are called to awaken. We who are lights against whirlwind and deception are called to be peacemakers: to make the dream of peace come true.

I open myself – I am immersed in presence. Life is living around me. Why should I recover from creation? So long as heart beats and I breathe, I gather and remember. Opening my eyes, this is you before me: a seeing person stands in being seen.

The dream of enlightenment does not come down to us. The dream is given while dream-maker remains hidden! Enlightenment becomes existentiated between us. Out of the soil of decency, dialogue emerges. I and Thou. Much depends now on how we nurture ourselves and engage one another.

To

To search for the identity of God (Goddess or God) without presumption, without a set prescription, independently, not dogmatically....

To walk in the dream of mirrors, through meanders of halls, through ornate chambers of the House of Spirit, the Baroque Long House of Spirit, and to follow footprints, traces of ancient gold amid mountains of cumulative dust; to discover fingerprints in the shaping of stuff, and to feel the breath, the breathing of eternal breath:

requires courage.

To experience presence, The Presence, even if but for the touch of that incomparable, ineffable moment, if but for the awe of a manifestation, revelation in a single glance, a gleam, a glimmering of light in motion out of non-light and borderless hush:

requires sensitivity and borderless empathy.

To be present in the world, flickering sphere of embers and ashes, the same startled and startling place of lamentation, alarms, and madness, yet to abide in reverence, turning toward the created and creating dynamics of who and what is other, otherness, and given:

requires commitment and clear perception.

To long with the warmth of openness, going among wounded and the lonely (even as an invitation goes to find those most in need of inviting) – always, everywhere mundane, seeking the Holy....

To be in this conflicting condition, these antithetical processes of existence, becoming existent, a conscious person in space (as in sacred space, space configurated for hallowing) and time (as with sacred time, duration circumscribed for awareness- sharing and power): every nexus along the space-time continuum, memorial where visible at the edge and invisible edging conjoins in trance-transfigurations, metamorphic visions, and mandala.

To make a poem....

To write a poem, poetry perhaps at best or at least one, once, perfect as a cherry blossom in a human palm or fruited bough a wind skirts through; to plant a tree a grove or an orchard; to bring forth a child or children into the wild and rainbows, and interspecies children of creation; doing what is done as acts of beauty, as generosity, as promissory righteousness:

requires integrity, and character too.

To be generous with beaconing, candling, tasting, feeding, to meditate and to flow – bright and big with cooking fire, calm and flushed as clean, salvific water....

To keep faith, that is, to trust, with a good mind and a good heart; to speak eloquently in honest dialogue from the unashamed and uncensored genius of your soul:

requires freedom of conscience.

To surrender to love, to atone, to at-one, desire and feel pain and elation, authenticating and liberating. Yet not to become a graveyard-silence; yet not to become the blood-shadow of a wall; never to spit upon or to destroy the miraculous kinships of the Earth, or to curse or spit into the faces of others. But to travel on as a young light, whether great or small, in wonderous, dappled fields of the living, across the unfathomable constellations of infinite light:

requires strength, imagination, and dignity.

To pray at prayers that walk, embracing the vulnerability of being human, and to walk a walk that prays – this is what is possible: this it best.

It requires courage.

Sufi

Each expression of beauty is an act of love. Every manifestation of love is an act of beauty.

To make a warrior's choice in the clarity of human evolution is to invite the flowering of beauty. To make a warrior's choice within the possibilities of wisdom is to work intimately in the garden of love.

A person does not need to define mystery to be transported to ecstasy. A person does not need to be a logician to join the poetry of dance.

Those with gnosis (and they are often spoken of plainly as Sufi) know these two, beauty and love, as one. In times like these they are those who make a warrior's choice; they chose the warrior's path. Fierce and tender is their love; of fire and water is glamour of their beauty.

Love's heroes delight to travel in the colors of the cosmic rainbow. The beautiful delight sharing the communion of radiance, as ordinary as the sharing of figs and bread, with friends and strangers alike.

These refined ones, sensitive to their cores (and they are often spoken of most plainly as Sufi) emerge into peopled places as troubadours. They play to uphold creation. They continue the story of life – the miraculous narrative of the miraculous universe growing constantly through orbs of self-observation and spheres of self-reflection.

Warrior-troubadours, vowed to love and beauty, speak truth

with a symmetry of humility and courage. Rapt in amazement, they come before those of us who are voiceless. They come before those of us who watch our shadows in the dust and have lost our music. Any moment dervishes and mandala dancers may reveal the heart as a mirror with wings!

Then, sheerly for the sake of giving, Sufis, the givers, restore breath to time; they soften what is hard; they sing the world. Not relics, certainly not statues, but as living presence, the Sufis bring peace to the afflicted and those tormented by fear. Light is extended to lives that have fallen, release made possible for the tortured and self-imprisoned.

A Sufi master might say to his followers, "If you desire to return to truth, remove the hard mask you are wearing. Be in search of the Face." Another might tell her friends, "The surest cure for corruption is laughter." At any moment, a Sufi may reveal the heart as a mirror with wings!

Why not then, since there is so much hurt and hunger in the human world, and so much trouble teeming throughout the Earth, come soon to the meeting of the finger and the thumb (where love and beauty have become one), and make a warrior's choice?

The Bard Exam

What is fire? Fire is passionate intensity. Fire has body. And the stronghold of fire is heart and blood.

What is water? Water is the flow of all that is, the mysterious, the miraculous, the metamorphic. To be one with fire and one with water, and to hold and be held by both is the Kingdom of Heaven, wedlocked with the Queendom of Earth.

What is air? The breath of life that issues from and returns to and issues again, in and out, endlessly, of the talking wind, this is air. The whisper – air, the tempest, laugh, the word, the sigh – air.

What is Earth? She is mother to all that lives, to all who have ever lived with and within her, here, in the great work of alchemic evolution. To all that is intimately known and sustaining of life – that is Earth, Earth-here, Earth-now. As far in all directions as the horizontal eye can see.

What is light? Ah! Light is the radiance of love. Light abides and is bestowed in cycles, in turnings, planetary revolutions, by sun, by moon, by stars. Light dwells in talking eyes, blossoms on lips against loneliness, providing guidance to the union of Heaven and Earth, revealed to the caring in the innocence of infants and in remembrance in the colored brilliance, bright-soft, of the arc of rainbow.

Aspirant, if you know the answers to these five druidic questions, then you know how to give birth to dreams, to Dreaming, to Time Out of Time, and know enough to sing the world.

The Everlasting Small

Even in the smallest experience: a bird on the branch of a tree in whatever season, a cup of tea and sounding of rain, one potato from that age-old land, a savory herb from out the gift of garden, a flower to caress a cheek and find the nostrils then the lips, too, the touch of a hand, the passing quickness of eye-beauty, colorful and lively-bright, entering eyes, deep silence of a snail pulling horns in from raindrops, the sigh of a sleeping infant, an infant's breath, a four legged friend, a solitary afternoon, or even a lighted candle in the slow hypnotic dance of candle flame, and more and more and so much there besides: is cause, in wealth, for gratitude.

For many yet and certain lands find heart's ease and comfort in what is small and full and blessed timelessly with freedom in the quietude that let's worry go and goes on without trouble or struggle, without shadow overhanging, or in fear. Not nearly enough bring it out into words and with childlike eagerness, wrapped prettily, to share, upending graveyards and the drear, dread culture of loneliness.

James Stephens once, partial to philosophy and Angus Og and gentleness and leprechauns, wrote a poem to Little Things, and Billy Yeats immortalized, countering the curse of progress, his longing-dream for the Lake Ilse of Innisfree. *"I will arise and go now..."*

Perhaps this is far too Romantic for a harried, hurrying, senseless, grabbing world? Ah then, but life loses its honey with no taste of romance and soon becomes, at center, gray emptiness where there is no poetry.

One need not be a poet either in a formal sense to keep a candle and a poem in the heart's treasure or honey on the tongue and sensory wonderment and defiance of the soul.

Once so long, so long ago, in full of night, I came upon a meditative newt, glistening black, entranced in full moonlight. Unheeding of my drawing near, the soft fleshed creature, in magic all her own, appeared to smile a euphoria signaling all being well within herself, between her body-place and the bestowing moon, and all well between us too.

That, in Once Upon a Time, a slow motion offering from the openness of being, was itself both a secret of life, in relationship, and down to the essence of poetry. The memory has not faded from me.

Man Walking an Unpaved Road

Man walks along an unpaved road. His feet make rhythm – the rhythm of a human walking (a two legged, as sages say). His feet form patterns on the wending road – changes to micro-climates and eco-structures, tiny thunders below the level of human hearing, miniature, momentary, storms of dust, the crunch and shuffle of boulder-pebbles. With every footfall a metamorphic happening.

Man looks round about. This day is fair, a soft day, and he silently thanks the day for its gentle kindness. No rain is hammering, wind is not rough, sun does not burn. Man looks round about, turning full circle to take his surroundings in: everywhere, encircling, he sees beauty, calm, beauty and life, filling place with the lushness of grass, in beadwork industry of ant hills, with scurrying of field mice at a glance and digging out of emerging, penny-weight shrews.

An energy of appreciation wells inside of man. He feels it upsurge and grow and swell in his chest, his throat; his hands like burning cauldrons of body-fire, a blush of blood-warmth coloring his cheeks. How can he contain this heat? He cannot! He is human.

Man stops. He begins to sing, singing the world as he finds it, as it, out and about in the encompassing circle of vision, enters and increases at a depth within him. Man on a road sings to Sky above; the solar, celestial mystery; to Earth below; the chthonic solidity; the dark power beneath his feet. He sings to the air he breathes (that has been breathed by myriad lives and forms before and will go on to be breathed again by others); breezing among clustered trees and solitary trees and bushes, berries, buds and leaves; swirling amid passing clouds and feeding birds, and birds in swift flight; to flowers in fields on either side of the unpaved road, Earth-stars growing from moist soil, showing delicate and many hued between stones, and also the man sings to the spirits of things and places. They the listeners, they the overseers – calligraphers of nature with miraculous pens and native brushes and inkwells of seasons.

Spirits are present, even when spirits appear to be absent; spirits are attentive even when staying silent – for they can, and they do feel. Here they absorb into elemental memory of Earth's archives man's singing appreciation, man's adoration, man's creature-joy that through their generosity has awakened, is arisen spontaneously inside his loving heart, poetized from depths of man's lyric soul.

Spirits of place are attentive (they are always attentive to participation and respect, to reverence for life, to honoring, or otherwise become alerted by indifference or intentions of hostility and invasiveness). Nothing is hidden in the Open and elementals are communicating masks and costumes of Being. Networks of spirit relationships are vibratory; are resonant. They manifest consciousness to observing consciousness on another level, at yet another frequency.

Those of this life-space, this place, where fulfilment of a man happens spontaneously on an unpaved road: spirits carry man's singing breath into dreaming realms, into dimensions of natural magic, kindred exchange, and ecstasy. In this democracy of experience is double gifting, binding creation, bringing visible and invisible into a moment's embrace of eternal unity.

This is dialogue, a dialogue of beauty, beauty and belonging. Belonging is the vulnerability of opening (being open to what is given, to what is, the vital surge of event mutuality) and beauty is nature's language of love.

Also, for tree, stone, a time, dust of a road, a human being in presence, person, man, woman, there is memory. Shadow of a tree is bestowal, shadow of being human, in this role, is blessing. Bestowal and blessing reach over generations, illuminating gatherings of ancestors and the wombs of progeny.

In Footsteps of the Wise

How much learning does a person need to be a human being; how much a human being to become a person? There are crossroads, thresholds, pivots, where native intelligence directs and we know in the immediacy of instinct what choices are right, what direction is optimal for life – worthy of the marvels of life and living with shared dignity.

We clutter our contemporary lives with information and lose and neglect the nourishment of truth and the guidance of necessity. In this overload there is spill over and we litter the world we inhabit. From the Age of Enlightenment to the Age of Information, the Living Earth becomes waste; the teeming Earth becomes landfill. The arboreal wonders, the venerable forests, lungs of the Earth, continue to vanish; the oceans are flotillas of plastic death.

Debris and lies are the burdens that wear out our minds and the possibilities of mindfulness. Debris and lies crush vitality from the soul and teach confinement and are the numbing chains of a civilization of false values and false pursuits, false expectations, and fatal betrayals.

A poem for a day and a meditation suffices. Moral character sustains inner evolution, is of key importance, and reverence for life is essential.

Look and listen carefully. Take time to observe and to feel and evaluate what is observed and what is felt. In the Open (at the threshold of Being) is power and mystery. In the All Around which is given is the antithetical, and awe and struggle and diversity.

This is Earth. Not one of us here has origin or ancestry at some extraterrestrial location. This place is a place of life. Earth is a Living Sphere. We are a species among species. And we are of the Earth.

Do you see how similar are the words "lie" and "life"? Remove a single letter and destroy the world. The same holds for extinctions – annihilate a species, destroy a world.

Make a prayer in the morning to give thanks for the thriving Earth, where you are active. Make prayer in the night to give thanks for the thriving Earth, where you rest.

Courage is essential to being human. Humility is as important as courage. We are Conscious Mortality and conduits of compassion. We are mobility and bearers of the dream of Freedom of Conscience.

Acclimate and acculturate yourself, your Eco-self, to response-ability. Life and lives depend on choices. Make a Warrior's Choice: walk lightly in the footsteps of the wise. Sit in the Council of All Beings; practice uniqueness of your Ecosophy (signature of your Earth Wisdom). Pursue peace and mutual respect and the return to sanity. Your priority is to be a lover.

Mother and Child

Of all visions accessible on this living Earth, no natural sight is more beautiful that a mother and child. If the mother and child are human (no matter of what race), they are beautiful.

If mother and child are lion or tiger, horse, bison, swan, or mountain sheep, beautiful.

If mother and child are bear, be they black or brown, grizzly, polar or panda, beautiful.

If mother and child are orcas or whales (from whatever pod the orcas, or whatever the type of whale), beautiful.

And on and on, throughout the visible enchantment of evolutionary diversity: Earth shares Her fecundity of magic and birthing miracles in patterns, cycles, and circles of rotating seasons.

Remember to re-member your existential disconnections back into Earth's biosphere of relationships: back to the immensity, intensity, and intimacy of nature.

Remember to think like a mountain, to grow inclusive and sustainable, horizontally vast, vertically profound, practicing patience and assuring habitation for ranging species and communities, nuanced shades of ecologic-identity and spiritually beneficent dreams.

The constancy of flowing water wears away the hardest monuments of imperial stone.

Live compassionately and find the Way with your uniqueness of welcome, passion and embrace. Return to walking in the Beauty Way. Return to traveling the Red Road of becoming appropriate and responsibly human.

As we emerge through time's emergency into the sacredness of maturity, we can release old views and the old need for clinging to transcendence. Deep in the numinous dialogue of maturity we learn to grow to the height of treetops, to trekking over rainbows, simultaneously rooting profound, and deeper still, into the ecosophy of the given and the open, and the narrative ancestry of where we came from, where we are and who we become along Earth's continuum from here.

When in the here and now and when we are reconnected through Earth and Cosmos to reverence for all life forms, with our souls we go immersed in the renaissance spirituality of *inscendence*. Then it is not to leave the Earth to find peace and plenitude in a hereafter, but to make peace flourish among us and attend, in trust and lovingkindness, the feast of inclusiveness, the banquet of biotic commensality.

Abide in the grounding dimension of natural creation. Abide via acts of beauty in rituals of community, communion, and affirmation, offering prayers as cultures of spontaneity, appropriateness, attunement and metamorphic reconciliation.

Return honoring to everyday activity. Sound the Orphic voice that subverts the shallow mind, plants visions of awakening in buried, sleeping souls. Bestow blessings of wakefulness. An open hand is a blessing. Magic in the language of eyes is a blessing. A blessing too is healing touch. Always the dignity of recognition. Making conditional the union of courage and gentleness.

Restore truth. From truth grows trust. Through trust dialogue flowers between us. Through dialogue, shell hardness cracks and possibilities break open. New life enters through opening.

To Earth, every mother is an Earth Mother, precious, nourishing, beautiful. Mothers respect this instinctual charge. To Earth, each child, a child of the Earth, is continuance, after its kind, renewal and beautiful. Children be birthed into belonging: honor, hallow, and love the gift of life. It is for you to become the beatitude of planetary future.

If you want to learn the way of the shaman, druid, alchemist, or sage, study the art of a tree. If you wish to experience the ecstasy of unknowing, go down to the ocean or recline in grass, with eyes upward, reflecting noiselessly on a starry sky in a cosmic night. If you desire to feel the sacred blessing of beauty without preparing to depart for the world hereafter, be at ease: look on a mother and child.

Other books in the Earth Spirit series

Belonging to the Earth
Nature Spirituality in a Changing World
Julie Brett
978-1-78904-969-5 (Paperback)
978-1-78904-970-1 (e-book)

Confronting the Crisis
Essays and Meditations on Eco-Spirituality
David Sparenberg
978-1-78904-973-2 (Paperback)
978-1-78904-974-9 (e-book)

Eco-Spirituality and Human–Animal Relationships
Through an Ethical and Spiritual Lens
Mark Hawthorne
978-1-78535-248-5 (Paperback)
978-1-78535-249-2 (e-book)

Environmental Gardening
Think Global Act Local
Elen Sentier
978-1-78904-963-3 (Paperback)
978-1-78904-964-0 (e-book)

Healthy Planet
Global Meltdown or Global Healing
Fred Hageneder
978-1-78904-830-8 (Paperback)
978-1-78904-831-5 (e-book)

Honoring the Wild
Reclaiming Witchcraft and Environmental Activism
Irisanya Moon
978-1-78904-961-9 (Paperback)
978-1-78904-962-6 (e-book)

Saving Mother Ocean
We all need to help save the seas!
Steve Andrews
978-1-78904-965-7 (Paperback)
978-1-78904-966-4 (e-book)

The Circle of Life is Broken
An Eco-Spiritual Philosophy of the Climate Crisis
Brendan Myers
978-1-78904-977-0 (Paperback)
978-1-78904-978-7 (e-book)

MOON
BOOKS

PAGANISM & SHAMANISM

What is Paganism? A religion, a spirituality, an alternative
belief system, nature worship? You can find support for all these
definitions (and many more) in dictionaries, encyclopaedias, and
text books of religion, but subscribe to any one and the truth will
evade you. Above all Paganism is a creative pursuit, an encounter
with reality, an exploration of meaning and an expression of the
soul. Druids, Heathens, Wiccans and others, all contribute their
insights and literary riches to the Pagan tradition. Moon Books
invites you to begin or to deepen your own encounter, right here,
right now.

If you have enjoyed this book, why not tell other readers by
posting a review on your preferred book site.

Medicine for the Soul
The Complete Book of Shamanic Healing
Ross Heaven
All you will ever need to know about shamanic healing and how to
become your own shaman...
Paperback: 978-1-78099-419-2 ebook: 978-1-78099-420-8

Shaman Pathways – The Druid Shaman
Exploring the Celtic Otherworld
Danu Forest
A practical guide to Celtic shamanism with exercises and
techniques as well as traditional lore for exploring the Celtic
Otherworld.
Paperback: 978-1-78099-615-8 ebook: 978-1-78099-616-5

Traditional Witchcraft for the Woods and Forests
A Witch's Guide to the Woodland with Guided Meditations and
Pathworking
Mélusine Draco
A Witch's guide to walking alone in the woods, with guided
meditations and pathworking.
Paperback: 978-1-84694-803-9 ebook: 978-1-84694-804-6

Wild Earth, Wild Soul
A Manual for an Ecstatic Culture
Bill Pfeiffer
Imagine a nature-based culture so alive and so connected,
spreading like wildfire. This book is the first flame...
Paperback: 978-1-78099-187-0 ebook: 978-1-78099-188-7